Lyrics for Re-Creation

Language for the Music of the Universe

James Conlon

Continuum • New York

1997

The Continuum Publishing Company
370 Lexington Avenue
New York, NY 10017

Printed in the United States of American.

Library of Congress Cataloging-in-Publication Data

Conlon, James, 1936-
    Lyrics for re-creation : language for the music of the universe /
James Conlon.
        p.   cm.
    Includes bibliographical references.
    ISBN 0-8264-0921-0
    1. Environmental education.   2. Environmentalism.   I. Title.
GE70.C66   1996
363.7—dc20   96-32593
                                                                              CIP

Grateful acknowledgment is made to Mambo Press for permission to
reproduce "A Movement" by Sally J. Timmel, from *Training for
Transformation: A Handbook for Community Workers*, vol. 3.

Lyrics for Re-Creation

*Language for the Music of
the Universe*

Contents

Dedication / 7
Introduction / 9
Prologue / 13

Embracing the Revelatory Moment
—*Earth Literacy* / 21
In the Beginning Was the Dream
—*The Dream* / 37
Unfolding Mystery and Meaning
—*The Story* / 45
Fueling Our Acts of Re-Creation
—*The Action* / 59
Free Beyond All Measure
—*Liberation* / 99
Epilogue
—*Soulwork for the New Millennium* / 111

Appendices
    A.   Action Autobiography / 117
    B.   I Have a Dream / 121
    C.   Project Earth / 123
    D.   Processes for Re-Creation / 125
Bibliography / 131
Notes / 139
Lyrics for Music of the Universe / 144

Dedication

Poetry is not a luxury, it is a vital necessity for our existence. It forms the quality of light from which we predicate our hopes and dreams toward survival and change, first into language, then into idea, then into more tangible action.
—Audre Lourde

The terminal decade of the century is becoming a moment of grace.
—Thomas Berry

The years following Vatican II have witnessed the rise of prophetic people, projects, and movements that have taken up the task of hope and harmony for all creatures on this fragile planet. *Lyrics for Re-Creation* provides words for the music of the universe. The people named below are among those whose work and lives have crafted such lyrics. It is to these prophetic people and their work that I dedicate these pages.

To the late Saul Alinsky and his many colleagues including Ed Chambers and Richard Harmon who continue the work of bringing the fire of hope out of the ashes of despair to urban and rural people in all parts of the globe.

To Paulo Freire, Sally Timmel and Anne Hope whose pedagogy of hope has brought courage and freedom to the oppressed of Latin America and to so many of us in the West.

To Gustavo Gutiérrez, Leonardo Boff, Ernesto Cardinale and all those who have articulated liberation theology as a gospel of freedom for oppressed people in Latin America and throughout the world.

To Rosemary Radford Ruether, Mary Hunt and so many others who have heightened our awareness of gender injustice and provided a better way through a feminist theology that is ecological and just.

To Thomas Berry, Matthew Fox, Brian Swimme, Sally McFague, Miriam MacGillis, Jay McDaniel and others who have given us a new vision of spirituality, ecology, and the cosmos.

To Gregory Baum, Robert McAfee Brown, Dorothee Soelle, Albert Nolan, Huston Smith, Jack Egan and others who have affiliated themselves with the movements emerging from their vision.

I wish to express my gratitude to all those who have contributed so generously to the preparation and publication of *Lyrics for Re-Creation: Language for the Music of the Universe.*

To Joan Marie LaFlamme, whose editorial efforts have contributed immeasurably to these pages.

To Rebecca Bier, Katherine Osborn, Marilyn Goddard, Lori Zook, and Cathryn Farrell, whose support and good work made the publication of this book a realizable goal.

To the students, faculty, and staff of the Institute in Culture and Creation Spirituality and the Sophia Center: Spirituality for the New Millenium, the Regional Connectors in Creation Spirituality, workshop participants, my colleagues at Holy Names College, my family and friends, and all those with whom I have shared the contents of this book.

To all those to whom I have listened and from whom I have learned, I am grateful.

Introduction

Jim Conlon's *Lyrics for Re-Creation* belongs to the culminating phase of the modern era of human history that began in 1543 when Copernicus discovered that Earth revolved around the Sun. As the radical investigations of modern science widened to include all forms of human knowledge, the worlds of belief and of action were never to be the same again. We all know the marvels of technology, and we are even grateful for much of this; but to appreciate the significance of Conlon's work, we must also be aware of what was lost with the birth of science.

Before the expansion of modern scientific knowledge, people everywhere awoke each day knowing where they were and what they were about. They began each day's work with a clear awareness that they lived at the center of the universe, in a place that God watched over and cared about, and they knew that their fundamental task was to live a good life so that at death they could join with the saints and angels and all others who had preceded them into heaven.

In one form or another, this story of the place and meaning of human existence was taught by at least some segment of humanity throughout the planet back for thousands of years. Each generation had learned the story from the preceding generation back into the mists of time. There are certainly important differences between the various stories told in the traditional cultures of the world, but when compared to the version of reality that modern science is teaching, these differences fade away.

During the four hundred years of its existence, modern scientific knowledge has enervated, crippled, or destroyed each and every traditional cosmology from all the civilizations of Earth. Certainly, science was not bent upon such destruction, at least not in the beginning. In its later stages of development, science did perhaps begin to breed minds intolerant of any claims to truths outside the domain of science. Such individuals did at times make a career of ridiculing and rebutting the truth-claims of other cultural traditions. But in the beginning, the first scientists were simply fascinated with this new way of investigating reality, and, overwhelmed by the volume of truth they were discovering, they had little time to notice one way or another whether their discoveries were at odds with the traditional accounts of reality recorded in the ancient books.

In the beginning, scientists were drawn into their lifelong search by the thrill of an original encounter with the greatness of being. They were uncovering truths that no one in all of human history, neither Aristotle nor Plato nor any other sage from the past, had ever before seen. If these truths were sometimes at odds with traditional cosmology, that was perhaps unfortunate for traditionalists, but it could not be helped. The deep satisfaction from such original encounters enabled the enterprise to continue and deepen, even if tensions inevitably arose when the new findings contradicted what people had believed forever.

The result was that science's new knowledge spilled out into the world without any deep relationship to the accrued wisdom of the ages. Apparently, the task of synthesizing the sciences with the religious traditions was beyond the capabilities or possibilities of that time. Where the scientists were too enthralled with their discoveries, the theologians were too defensive. Unable to assimilate this knowledge, many religious thinkers backed away as if to protect themselves from a fatal virus. But however difficult the challenge might have been, it will always be the case that ignoring the wisdom that has proved its value over time is an extremely risky move. And soon enough, the entire enterprise has become disastrous, as scientific knowledge, translated into technology, simply overwhelmed the human and life communities.

If we were to bring back even the most trenchant critics of the modern scientific culture and plop them down in our world, they would all be profoundly stymied by the enormity of what is taking place in the twentieth century. As Conlon details in several places, enormous technological power wielded by a single species without cosmological wisdom is degrading life everywhere. But even at this nadir of human history, a remarkable reversal has begun to take place. After science has roamed about destroying the traditional cosmologies throughout every continent, it is now beginning to be assimilated into a new cosmological wisdom.

No one expected science to become a wisdom tradition, least of all the scientists themselves. Their business was knowledge of the universe without any concern about whether this was supportive of or contradictory to the meanings of human existence as articulated by the religions of the world. It is hard to imagine that such a program, carried out with a vengeance, would ever mature into a new wisdom tradition.

Perhaps only William Blake remains undisturbed. Although he hated Newtonian science as the scourge of humanity, he also held that if one persists long enough in one's folly, one will eventually achieve wisdom. In our own time, we are seeing just this transformation from folly to wisdom take place as science discovers the "bionic unity" and seamless integrity of the entire Earth and universe.

We have before us the possibility for a radically new orientation in the universe, and it is precisely this possibility that Jim Conlon has seized upon. He takes as his fundamental context the new cosmology as articulated by Teilhard de Chardin, Thomas Berry, and others, a synthesis of the evolutionary universe as discovered by science with the sacred universe as understood by our spiritual traditions. Conlon's passion throughout his work is to find the ways in which we can live and act so that the stories of our lives can once again become congruent with the Great Story of the universe.

For Conlon, an understanding of the new cosmology is only a first step. What is profoundly necessary is a reinvention of our lives, our actions, and our institutions so that we can enter into our true roles in this sacred universe. Conlon explores practical strategies in the work of education, community organizing, environmental action, psychology, and cultural reinvention with this aim of invoking a new era of humanity, one he calls the ecological age.

To understand the significance of Conlon's work, we must begin with an awareness that the explosion of modern scientific knowledge, which resulted in so much destruction, is now being assimilated into a new cosmology and a new wisdom. If, in contradistinction from our ancestors, we are not yet able to awaken with an awareness of where we are and what we are to do for our salvation, it is only because the journey from one story to another is an immense one. However, our homecoming is closer now than at any time during the last four hundred years, and, with Conlon's *Lyrics for Re-Creation*, we are able to take yet another step toward our shared destiny, deep liberation, and profound fulfillment.

—Brian Swimme

Prologue — The Human Venture

The spirit sleeps in the stone, dreams in the flower, and becomes awake in humanity.

—Leonardo Boff[1]

No revolutionary movement is complete without its poetic expression. If such a movement has caught hold of the imagination of the masses, they will seek to vent in song the aspirations, fears and hopes, the loves and hatreds, engendered by the struggle. Until the moment is marked by the joyous, defiant singing of revolutionary songs, it lacks one of the most distinctive works of a popular revolutionary movement; it is the dogma of the few and the faith of the multitude.

—James Conolly[2]

People today are living in shanty towns from Rio de Janeiro to New York City. Alienated expatriots from Mexico, Central America, and Cuba walk the streets of Los Angeles and Miami in fear. Young parents face a possible lifetime of unemployment because of the collapsed economies of Dublin, Sheffield, and Chicago. High school children become welfare recipients and unwed parents in the neglected tenements of our inner cities. Children in Brooklyn and Vancouver learn about drugs, violence, and death instead of experiencing the enchantment of love or the wonder of belonging.

There is so much pain and violence in the streets. High school students are wounded on their graduation day; women are raped in their homes; waterways are polluted with spilled oil; the land absorbs poisonous fertilizer. The many forms of devastation signify profound denial of the limits of the human condition. The consumer madness of the shopping mall is one representation of the reluctance to live within these limits. Ecological devastation is in many ways an expression of rage against the human condition, a rage against limits, which is played out as a rage against Earth.

How can we heal Earth and its people? What lies before us is the invitation and the power to create, to celebrate the sacredness of life in its many forms. We need a new Earth community in which we can discover sacredness, meaning, self-understanding, and hope. As Boutros Boutros Ghali, the Secretary General of the United Nations, said at the 1990 Earth Summit, "Henceforth the future of the world is in our hands."

In light of pathology and oppression, and the magnitude of the task before us, I ask this question. Is it possible to engage in meaningful action in a manner that is: (1) congruent with our world view; (2) true to our vision of the future; (3) aligned with the unfolding of our lives; (4) creative and transformative for all participants; and (5) also mutually enhancing for humans and the natural world? I propose that the answer is Yes, and that it is possible through a process of Earth literacy, dream, story, action, and liberation. What follows is an introduction to this process.

Earth Literacy

Lyrics for Re-Creation begins with Earth literacy. Seeing Earth in a new way, we realize that as humans we are as much Earth as are the rocks, water, and trees. With new eyes, we embrace all life as sacred and celebrate depth, beauty, and diversity in all that is. We come to understand that there is a revelatory dimension in the material world, that the Divine communicates to us through all aspects of creation. We listen and respond; we find our voice and speak our word into every dimension of life. Earth literacy empowers us to grasp the significance of each moment, "to read the signs of the times." In this way, we discover a new perception of identity, destiny, and purpose. Earth literacy challenges us to restore Earth and restructure society. Our journey culminates in the liberation of Earth and all its peoples, a liberation that is both interior and systemic. In this process, we are freed of any internal obstacles and liberated from any structures that would oppress people or devastate the planet.

The Dream

The movement from literacy to liberation is fueled by a dream—a dream that is revolutionary, utopian, and new; a dream of a resacrilized culture where reciprocity is fostered and reverence restored; a dream of energy, union, and magnetic intuition that allures us, motivates us, and draws us forward into action; a dream that tomorrow can be better than today. This multifaceted dream exerts a profound attraction that propels us to action. In that action, our dream becomes the dream of Earth.

The Story

Telling our stories is essential as we strive to bring our dreams into action. Storytelling makes freedom possible as we discuss who we are and where we are going. Stories build bridges between our dreams and our actions.

Carl Jung's statement "the dream drives the action" is profoundly true. It has been ratified in the lives of many people. In an interview shortly before his death, baseball Hall of Famer Mickey Mantle said, "All I ever wanted to be was a ball player." As he looked back on his life, he could say that he had realized his dream.

Singer and songwriter John Lennon articulated his dream when he wrote in the lyrics of "Imagine" the following: "Imagine all the people living in peace."

Dorothy Day, cofounder of the *Catholic Worker*, followed a dream of serving the poor by providing food and shelter and by a life of voluntary poverty.

The Rev. Martin Luther King, Jr., had a dream of racial justice and nonviolence. And Pope John XXIII had a dream of openness and renewal whereby the gospel would touch the lives of all people of good will.

It is their stories—and ours—that have and will make this a better world for the children. Stories name the transformational events that constitute our journey. From this perspective, the universe is a story, too, a galactic story, an Earth story, a life story, a human story. As we understand this Earth story through science, experience it in our spiritual practice, and express it in creative form, we fashion a new context for our lives. We discover that the story of the universe and our story are not separate. This awareness leads to greater and greater consciousness and freedom; we discover who we are and what we are called to do.

In our storytelling, we celebrate difference, depth, and interdependence. We discover the psychic dimension of all creation. We connect in a new way to the unexpected powers of creativity and new life that reside in the recesses of each of us. We dissolve the boundaries between the inner world and the outer world.

Action

Action focuses our efforts; it tests our values and achieves results. Organizing and storytelling help us take our stories into action. We tell our stories in the context of the universe story and act in harmony with Earth. We understand that Earth is speaking and acting through us.

This process brings us hope, courage, and creativity; it fosters communication, relationship, and listening. We embrace paradox, follow our hearts, and practice recognition through multiple phases of organizing: *pre-organizing*, building relationships; *disorganizing*, dissolving oppressive patterns; *organizing*, creating new structures; and *reorganizing*, moving toward transformation.

The process of change is a great adventure in education. Earth becomes our classroom as we ourselves become part of the change we want to see in the world. Through deep learning, we achieve competence for our role in the unfolding story. The process is liberating and organic, although we may undergo loss and dislocation as we reflect on the world in order to transform it. Deep ecology and green economics provide additional resources for actions in and through Earth.

Our new view will provide a more integral relationship with the Earth community. This experience of interconnectedness and intimacy will foster, in turn, meaningful action. Through promoting relationships, reflection, and self-discovery, we move forward to resolve the great—and small—issues of our time through new levels of partnership and cooperation: the formation and development of a coalition for Earth.

Liberation

The challenged of liberation is to provide hope for future generations, to embrace "the wellspring that we dare to call our life" (Teilhard de Chardin).[3] To engage fully in the process of freedom, "we return to the forest and remember the lessons learned on the pathway to the moon" (Loren Eisley).[4] Liberation fosters the rebirth of culture and the practice of justice for Earth and all creation (geo-justice) through mutually supportive relationships between humans and all creation.

Liberation involves seeing the world differently, being able to dream again, telling the story of the universe and our own stories, and organizing them into actions that are ecological and just. These actions will meet the needs of the present without compromising the ability of future generations to meet their own. They will flow out of literacy, dream, and story. Liberation involves achieving the freedom necessary to support the integrity of creation and restructuring society to support life, especially the lives of the weakest and most endangered.

In my previous writing, I have attempted to name a perspective from which to work toward social and ecological justice. Through listening to the story of Earth, we see that there are three primary tendencies in all of life: *communion, differentiation,* and *interiority.*[5] In *Geo-Justice: A Preferential Option for Earth,* I explored the cultural implications of these through examining three components of geo-justice: global (communion), local (differentiation), and psychosocial (interiority). In my more recent work, *Earth Story, Sacred Story,* I deepened the reflection on the trinitarian quality of all of life. I propose that geo-justice and a spirituality of Earth require an intimate connection with these primary dynamics. I offer the following as another way to reflect on these three principles: connection and compassion (communion), creativity and uniqueness (differentiation), and subjectivity and depth (interiority).

In these writings, I propose that geo-justice and cultural rebirth are a personal and planetary call to discover the converging terrain between ecological and social justice, a passionate and practical challenge to participate in the harmony, balance, and peace Earth already knows (but that are threatened by humans who "have eyes but do no see; ears but do not hear"). In this work, I hope to provide a trinitarian approach that will result in an awareness of the Divine Presence as it gives birth to sacredness from among and outside existing forms and becomes a sacrament for the era that is ours to create.

The earlier works provide the landscape and framework for the "seamless garment" of social and ecological justice; *Lyrics for Re-Creation* offers a guide for accomplishing the task. I believe that if we reflect on the themes offered in each of the chapters (Earth Literacy, Dream, Story, Action, Liberation), we will be able to engage in the work of the new creation, the great work of restoring Earth and restructuring society to further balance and peace. Each chapter in *Lyrics for Re-Creation* is composed as a movement in the great cosmic symphony: Embracing the Revelatory Moment, In the Beginning was the Dream, unfolding Mystery and Meaning, Fueling Our Acts of Re-Creation, and Free Beyond All Measure are language for the music of the universe.

Twelve Blessings

In preparation for learning to sing lyrics to accompany God's music for Earth, I want to share the beautiful poem *Twelve Blessings,* by Brother David Steindl-Rast, OSB,[6] a man fluent in the language of the universe. For me, it combines dream and myth (story), the endless blessings and harmony of Earth, and the divine love of the Creator of all.

Twelve Blessings

Twelve blessings for the twelve months of the young
year to come—twelve angels to guard and guide you.

When the Wolf Moon grows fat
and the North Wind roars on the shore,
an angel shall feed your fire
and bolt your door.

When the Clean Spring Moon rises,
an angel, unheard and unseen,
shall clean your seven springs
and keep them clean.

When the Sap Moon draws sap
upwards from bulb and root,
an angel gardener shall guard
each new green shoot.

When the Grass Moon makes grasses
nod to each other in bloom,
an angel in white shall greet you
at the bright empty tomb.

When the Planting Moon mirrors
her face in the cold frame glass,
an angel shall breathe at your seedlings
till all frosts pass.

When the Rose Moon blooms
in the sky like a silver-wrought rose,
an angel shall show you a rose garden
no one else knows.

When a frolicsome angel
rolls the Hay Moon over the hill,
you shall dance with the deer in the dark
while time stands still.

When the Green Corn Moon glides
through the ripening corn, row by row,
an angel shall make swelling spikes
sweet as they grow.

When the Harvest Moon lantern
hangs golden and plump in the sky,
you shall hear an angel's scythe zing.
You won't ask why.

When the Hunter's Moon races
black clouds like a galloping prince,
an angel shall draw his bow,
yet, you won't wince.

When the Frosty Moon blinds
every pond with a thin film of white,
eeling scales from your eyes, an angel
shall heal your sight.

When the Long Night Moon wanes
and the darkness keeps deepening fast,
an angel shall forge from your fears
faith that will last.

Embracing the Revelatory Moment
—Earth Literacy

A growing number of scientists and scholars tell us that it is essential to master a new level of literacy. Without it, we can't create a civilization that makes sense, planetary sense, cosmic sense. The literacy we must master is Earth literacy.

—McGregor Smith[1]

As children, we explore the world around us by curiosity and questioning; when we experience something new, we ask "What's that?" Behind our question is the quest to name, understand, and engage with—to be literate. Have you visited a country where your language was not spoken? I recall being in Mexico, Colombia, and the province of Quebec, unable to understand or be understood. I was cut off from normal communication with others. These were painful and alienating experiences, because communication is central to being human. Communication reveals who we are; it is through relationship that we know and are known. Not only do we need to be understood, but we need to understand. Furthermore, we need to extend this understanding to our planet. Unfortunately, we live in a culture that refuses to communicate with Earth. Seven of the warmest years on record have occurred in the last decade, for example, and yet we refuse to discuss global warming or take steps to prevent it. This autism is attributable, in large part, to the mechanistic worldview that has separated spirit from matter and humans from Earth.

We need to develop a language with the natural world that takes us beyond identification *of* and into identification *with*. We need to establish a relationship that perceives Earth as not *mine* but *me*. This language can be called *Earth literacy*.

Such language enables us to comprehend our world and our place in it. As people of different traditions, we can see that our spiritual journey is, in fact, a journey into literacy with Earth. Jay McDaniel develops the image of a common voyage across a river. There are different ways to proceed. There is the raft—the Christian raft moving toward the reign of God; the Jewish raft sailing toward Shalom; and the Islamic raft pursuing Paradise. The rafts are accompanied by canoes occupied by the indigenous peoples—the Native American, Inuit, African, Australian, European—those close to Earth. There are also swimmers, those who have jumped off the rafts or been pushed. Everyone, whatever his or her vehicle for crossing, realizes that this is a common journey. Together, they notice that the river, the context of their common journey, is polluted. In this story, of course, the river is Earth.[2]

FOR REFLECTION

Take a few moments to consider the following points adapted from the work of Carolyn Merchant in *Radical Ecology*.[3]

Sense of place
Where did you grow up?
What do you remember about your relationship to the land?
When was the last full moon?
What was the rainfall last year?
When was the last natural disaster in your area?
Name five native plants.
Where does your garbage go?
What species have become extinct in your area?

Reverence for life
Describe your experience of a warm relationship with a nonhuman creature.

Allegiance to the planet
Do you feel a commitment to protecting the natural resources and rhythms of your particular part of the planet?

Cosmic awe
Describe a time you have felt the awe and mystery of Earth.

Listen and be with
How often do you set aside time to be with Earth?

These aspects of Earth literacy remind us that we are but a small part of a large world.

Increasing our ability to communicate with Earth provides us with a sense of power. This power is not the traditional power *over* something, with its connotations of domination and manipulation, but a strength rising from within and around, power *among* other things. Common to us all, this strength is often symbolized by a circle. This is the power drawn on when people gather together in groups as equals, whether in women's or men's circles, round tables, sweat lodges, or drumming circles. In communication with Earth and one another, we not only *know* our calling, we *feel* it.

Earth literacy makes intimacy more possible, intimacy both with other humans and with the natural world. Through this new intimacy, we further increase our awareness, sensitivity, and capacity to listen; strengthened in our relationships, we experience an increased capacity to act. And in our actions, we draw closer to our deeper purpose and call.

Earth literacy brings us into deeper contact with ourselves. This awareness was articulated by John Muir, who wrote, "I only went out for a walk and finally concluded to stay until sundown, for going out, I discovered I was going in." Earth literacy deepens our awareness of our interior experience. With psychologist Carl Jung, we come to understand that "the galaxies within are as great as the galaxies without."

Another level of Earth literacy is communication with the divine. The fourteenth-century mystic Meister Eckhart points out: "All creatures are words of God." When we increase our awareness of Earth, we increase our awareness of the Divine. We acknowledge each creature as a manifestation of the Divine, a reminder of the sacredness that permeates all creation.

One of my learnings related to Earth literacy comes from my earliest years growing up on the banks of the St. Clair River in the southwestern region of Ontario, Canada's central and most populated province. I remember being taught to read the book of nature and to savor the revelatory moments that poured into my consciousness and flooded my soul in so many wonderful ways. Among these recollections are the delicious taste of raspberries that grew in the garden, the stately maple that provided sap and syrup in the spring, and leaves to play in during the fall. The majestic St. Clair, home to pickerel, perch, bass, and smelt, carried Great Lakes freighters in her channel and cooled eager swimmers on hot summer days. The river is my fondest recollection.

The new potatoes and fresh tomatoes from my father's garden and my mother's culinary gifts, manifest in rhubarb pies, are memories that connect me to the place on the planet where I was a boy. Memories of the evening rain on the roof in springtime and the first snow that carpeted our village in early winter come flooding back. Memories of these intimate moments with people and the natural world taught me much about Earth literacy. These recollections of tastes and smells, flora and fauna, summer days and winter nights, sunrises and night skies, friends, family, and roots move me deeply and remind me of the longing for belonging and the experience of home. They remind me of the importance of being connected and of the capacity that each of us has for love and literacy with humans and the natural world.

So, the other side of Earth literacy is the expression of ourselves. This communication involves declaring our identity and living our realizations of oneness with Earth. My own adult experience of Earth literacy came through such a step. I knocked on a door in Toronto's East End, introduced myself to the young couple who replied, and asked if they had any concerns about their neighborhood. They invited me in and voiced their anxieties about pollution. In the backyard, they pointed out the carbon ash on the freshly washed clothes and drew my attention (hardly necessary!) to the odor from a tanning factory on the shores of Lake Ontario. Returning outside, I asked whether they would attend a meeting to discuss these issues in the neighborhood church the following week; their answer was, "Yes."

Other neighbors were also willing. They gathered and told their stories. They decided on an action. Two weeks later, the young couple led a delegation to the president of the tanning factory, who agreed to enforce the environmental standards. Immediately, there was a significant reduction of ash and odor in the neighborhood. The awareness of pollution led to community actions to eliminate it, and, in the process, the people of the neighborhood discovered their own power.

As humans, we are all challenged to participate fully and creatively in Earth/human relations. This participation involves moving into action, as the group in Toronto did. Our task is to restore ecological balance and restructure political and economic relationships on local and global levels. We have the potential to transform our society and restore our planet, but we must transcend old ways of thinking and align our actions with the dynamics of the natural world. We must learn to participate in life on Earth rather than try to dominate or manipulate it. As James Berry who edits a newsletter on the new cosmology says, "We will see Earth as one integrated system—so we can, at last, make sense out of our relationships and give every aspect of the entire system its due."

To do so, we need to draw on the resources of both ancient wisdom and modern science to transform our hearts and minds and, in turn, the region of Earth we call home. The recognition by science of a bionic unity has confirmed the experience of the mystics. There are patterns of order residing beneath this seemingly chaotic surface. As we learn to see these patterns, we recognize life to be a complex and ongoing process. The conviction that disorder will eventually achieve a new order is an important perspective from which to view cultural change. For example, it helps us understand that the turbulence resulting from change in the church or Black Power or feminism or gay rights is yet another form of story. These stories lead to actions, which, when properly responded to, will result in racial equality, gender justice, and dignity for all.

Yet, each evening the news reminds us of the enormous assault on difference that is taking place on our world stage. The term "ethnic cleansing" is nothing but a euphemism for racism and injustice, whether in Bosnia, Ireland, or our urban ghettos. Violence and injustice remian rampant in our midst. Father Bill Callahan of the Quixote Center in Maryland proposes that we should pray the news in order to realize that the crucifixion continues, that to accept and celebrate difference is perhaps our greatest challenge.

Still, Earth literacy is a new way to read and write, to reflect on and act out our relationship to the natural world. Geo-justice offers us a new way to live in harmony with Earth. Geo-justice embraces social and ecological justice; it reminds us that the crack in the ozone layer is directly related to the crack sold on the street. Geo-justice expands the preferential option for the poor to the preferential option for Earth. Earth becomes the reference point for our action, the perspective from which we enter into relationships of harmony, balance, and peace with all creation.

This vision becomes a compelling context for the imaginative and creative work of transformation. What are we called to contribute? One step in answering this question is to see what we have already contributed, to create an *action autobiography* focused on social and ecological justice. Doing so gives us an opportunity to reflect upon both the oppression and the inspiration in our lives, to review the actions we have taken thus far, and to make connections between our awareness and our actions. An action autobiography provides an opportunity for us to look back to where we have been and forward toward possibilities for the future. It provides the opportunity for praxis; through action, reflection, and new action, we act ourselves into a new way of thinking and think ourselves into a new way of acting. We are confronted with important questions and have the opportunity to explore their implications for our lives.

An Action Autobiography on Behalf of Earth

Start writing your own action autobiography. Responding to specific questions may help you begin. Select those that are helpful from the list below.

- What is your earliest recollection of an action in which you tried to bring about change? How was this action a statement of hope and courage? A confrontation with resignation and inertia? How did your action result in increased solidarity with others? Did this action increase your belief in people as a source of action on behalf of freedom, equality, and peace?
- What do you need to learn in order to foster your awareness of Earth?
- What people bring you hope or promote freedom or courage or compassion?
- What has been your most prophetic effort on behalf of Earth?
- What universal principles do you believe in and how do they serve to guide your work?
- In what ways have you worked toward unity between your awareness of Earth and your actions for it?
- What have you learned about yourself and Earth through your efforts?
- What continues to hold you back? How are you engaged with the forces of oppression, the symbols and sources of limitations in your life?
- What have you seen, felt, or done to increase your capacity to bring about change? What do you intend to do?
- How have your efforts toward geo-justice and liberation deepened your experience of the Divine?
- What do you see as the next phase of your journey?
- What components of geo-justice inform your vision of the future?

Excerpts from my own action autobiography are provided in Appendix A. You may find the material—my story—useful as you formulate your own.

Our action autobiography sets our agenda for today and illuminates our vision for tomorrow. The next sections of this book reflect on the meaning of dream, story, and action in achieving our goals.

Having reflected on our dreams and told our stories, we next look beyond ourselves to put those stories in a greater context and then into action: we listen to the story of the universe. The story provides a wonderful weaving of mystery and meaning. The story that currently operates in the culture has resulted in enormous pathology. It is clear that this story must change and be replaced by the new story of the universe; the story that carries within it a powerful potential for life.

At Genesis Farm in New Jersey, and other Earth literacy programs around the world, educators are bringing forth approaches to evoking the story. Through an increased sensitivity to beauty, emotion, mystery, and metaphor, they proclaim and celebrate the universe as a single creative act. Increasingly, they are celebrating this event as a moment of grace in our time.

The cosmic story can, and should, be a framework for creating culture. When honored, the universal principles of *differentiation, subjectivity,* and *communion* provide context, meaning, and direction for our lives.

Differentiation

> The universe comes to us as a totality where each being and each moment announces this thrilling news: I am fresh. To understand the universe you must understand me.[4]

Differentiation honors the fact that every person, stone, tree, and animal is a unique creation. Indeed, the universe thrives on diversity. Learning not only to tolerate but to respect our differences, both individual and cultural, is crucial to the work of liberation. Differentiation provides multiple sources from which solutions to our problems are found.

> You are the sound of all that needs new definition, or new meaning, of all that gurgles in the womb of time waiting to be born.
> —Catherine de Vinck

Interiority

> The universe consists of subjects—centers of sentience and spontaneity.[5]

Subjectivity or *interiority* means we each have a personality that is our own, a spontaneous energy that creates relationships. This self-organizing principle comes out of the depth of energy that is uniquely us. Interiority reminds us of our profound capacity for deep experience, self-expression, and relationship. Interiority reminds us that everything has a voice; it tells you who it is by its structure and organic process.

> And I do hear the summons hidden within the miracle of stone, then I can name the holy, the fire within, the fire of all things.
> —Catherine de Vinck

Communion

> To be is to be related.... Much of our existence finds fulfillment in relatedness.

Communion means we are all related. We are one, although we are many; we are together, although we are apart. We honor the wisdom of the late scientist David Bohm, who reminded us that science teaches that there is no basis for separation. Communion invites us to celebrate and participate in the unity and interconnectedness of the universe.

> Maples! I am gripped by an intense yearning to see you, to greet you, to touch you, to be touched by you.
> —Maple Ecstasy

In my work, I have come to see that these three principles must be present in the culture if geo-justice is to be present. Differentiation respects our diversity. We are human and nonhuman; male and female;

black, brown, red, white, and yellow. We are multiple aspects of the Divine. Interiority is the psychic as well as the spiritual dimension through which we embrace the sacred depths of all creation. Communion heals the alienation in life, the separateness present among nations and people, and invites us to embrace our common unity as planetary citizens.

The relationship between this new view of ourselves and our universe (the new cosmology) and cultural change can be understood as the dialectic between two forces: the force of gravitation and the force of expansion. Gravitation can be seen as the energy of containment, the force that represents tradition and continuity of what is salvageable from the past. At the same time, it both honors our history and sheds new light on it. It represents the ancient wisdom of the scriptures, the medieval mystics, and the writings of early theologians.

The energy of expansion expresses the new insights of science, art, and approaches to action and change. These are represented in psychic research; the implications of chaos theory, fractals, and parapsychology; and the most recent insights into how the new cosmology can influence the culture. These and other expressions of discontinuity represent the threshold experiences of novelty and innovation. The dynamic between gravitation and expansion creates the unfolding dynamic of the universe; the resulting trajectory has been named by Thomas Berry the "curvature of compassion." This "compassionate curve" embraces us in the same way a mother embraces a child.

In *My Quest for Beauty,* Rollo May says, "In our creativity we destroy and rebuild the world and at the same time we inevitably rebuild and reform ourselves." We are affected by our actions. We cannot say that we are going to transform our parish, our school, or our community and be exempt from transforming ourselves. We rebuild our own lives as we rebuild our society.

One way of transforming our lives is by creating new myths, new explanations of our reason for being. Or, as Sam Keen says, we work to make our unconscious myths conscious. To do so, we take the constellations of feelings, thoughts, and experiences from "inside" and put them "outside." Keen's idea is to find out what really drives us and how accurate or necessary it is. If we create our symbols in alignment with the principles of the universe and the dynamics of Earth, they will be truly powerful. We are not following the Newtonian paradigm of shifting matter and form but rather reshaping energy into healthy relationships. We are rereading our own stories and, when necessary, rewriting them in accord with the cosmic story.

As a participant in Earth literacy program "Exploring the Sacred Universe" at Genesis Farm in New Jersey, I felt that what I have studied and written about was actually being lived out. From biodynamic gardening to wholesome organic food, to the study of the new story in workshops and field trips to experience the bioregion, I felt a deep joy in knowing that I was participating in living out a "functional cosmology." I felt a deep joy in experiencing a congruence between the new world view (the new story) and the manner in which it was being practiced in relationship to the natural world, to people, and to the Divine. I remember writing to Thomas Berry to tell him how excited I felt in seeing his vision being brought into practice. It was a source of encouragement for each of us that we, too, can have a story and bring it into practice.

Cultural genesis becomes, when all is said, a rebirth of images and myths, a rebirth of life inside and outside existing cultural forms. It is an awakening to the interconnectedness of all things in solidarity with Earth and an expanding universe pulsating with life. Culture is not split from nature but is an expansion of it. If integrated with nature's cycles and patterns, culture can grow from Earth as an apple grows from the tree.

Literacy and Liberation

When Vice President Al Gore wrote *Earth in Balance,* motivated by a near-tragic accident. His nine-year-old son was hit by a car as the family was leaving a Baltimore Orioles baseball game. Although his son recovered, the incident deepened Gore's awareness of a collision happening on a larger level: the collision between Earth and some of its people, resulting in vast devastation of the natural world. The event that endangered his son's life moved him to call for ecological awareness. His efforts have resulted in many people caring for Earth in unprecedented ways. Gore's vision is revealed in these words: "Conserve hope, manage fear, recycle wonder, use technology without being subservient." In his writings and in his life, Gore has joined an ever-increasing circle of those inviting us to a new Earth literacy. He is one of a chorus of voices working to move us first to awareness and then to action, understanding that Earth literacy is not just something you study but something you do.

The Grandmother Project in southern Florida began when a group of older women became concerned about the ecological legacy that was being passed on to their grandchildren. As they came together to reflect on these global problems, they realized that humans had gotten offtrack and were on the verge of bankrupting our planet and putting human life itself at risk. Realizing this, they decided to prepare a profit-and-loss statement for the Gross Earth Product. Wanting to embrace the "big picture," they decided to extend their research and study to cover the last hundred million years! In their two-year project, they studied, took courses, read, and compiled files and charts. They achieved an understanding of energy consumption, resource use, population impact, and more. The results of this project revealed that over the last hundred tbmillion years, Earth demonstrated an ever-increasing capacity to support life, but in the last 150 years, that trend has been reversed! As Buckminster Fuller wrote, "Humans are hooked on a game of life that has nothing to do with the way the universe is going."

The culmination of the project was the preparation of reports that took many forms but shared a common theme: the situation is urgent. Each report pointed to the necessity for us to begin again to reconstruct the conditions for a healthy Earth and arrest the current plunge toward ecological bankruptcy. For their final meeting, the grandmothers were joined by a group of fourteen-year-olds from a nearby junior high school. As the reports were given, one student was asked whether he would have preferred to live at an earlier time when all was harmony and peace or at this time of the "downward plunge." His answer was that he preferred to live at this present moment, saying, "We know now. What are we going to do about it?" His question calls for a quantum shift into a new pattern of human/Earth relationship.

This shift involves the restoration of our planet. We need to deepen the capacity to coexist with as little negative impact as possible. We need to use our technological genius for the good of Earth. The work involves entering the natural world in a manner that fosters deep inner transformation and communion. We need to see Earth as an evolving community to which we are intimately related.

A literacy that moves us to restore Earth is always grounded in the context in which we live. This includes our racial background, sexual identity, economic status, and the bioregion in which we live. When we respond to political and economic oppression or ecological devastation, community inevitably results. In fact, it has been my experience over the years that community is always a byproduct of struggle and celebration, not an end in itself. When community happens through our engagement in the struggle to restructure political and economic oppression and restore ecological devastation, we find that we face the future with an increased sense of interconnectedness. Our experience in the struggle heals the fragmentation that so permeates our culture.

This reality was well named by Robert Bellah and his associates in *Habits of the Heart*. They point out that the abundance of therapy in North American life is motivated by the need to heal the alienation that people feel. The basis of this experience is found at the deepest level in our alienation from Earth. Central to our experience of this deep-seated alienation from Earth is the chasm that exists between our understanding of nature and culture. Today, that chasm is being healed as our awareness extends beyond what Alan Watts called the "skin-encapsulated ego" to the "ecological self," that dimension of our being that extends its identification to the natural world. We come to see, remember, and know our neighborhood, city, or bioregion with its trees, water, air, land, sunlight, and people. In this way, we recognize a profound interconnectedness with ecological systems. This recognition leads us to respond to an attack on the natural world around us in the same way that we would respond to an attack on our physical selves. We can say with John Seed of the Rainforest Action Project in Australia, "I am the rainforest protecting myself."

On a cultural level, this awareness of the other is understood as solidarity, the bonding that occurs among people who respond to a common experience of oppression. This solidarity happens when we overcome, for example, social injustice, gender inequality, or economic disparity.

When ecological self and cultural solidarity converge, a new relationship to Earth emerges, one that heals the split between nature and culture, between planet and people. We have brought the connection with the human (solidarity) and a deeper relationship with the natural world (ecological self) into one act. The result is a holistic experience of Earth literacy. Being fully literate liberates us from the internal blocks of despair and energizes us to overcome political, economic, cultural, and ecological oppression.

One of the most inspiring phrases I have read is Gustavo Gutiérrez's statement in *The Green Bible:* "Creation is the first act of liberation." Liberation is the intention of creation. When things come into existence, they bring with them the inherent right to fulfill that existence. Liberation is worked out in history, those transformational moments that mark the unfolding of the natural world (the birth of galaxies, planets, life on Earth, and human epochs), as well as the sequence of events recounted in politics, economics, and culture. Understood in this way, liberation becomes the process of continuing the great evolutionary work of all creation.

As humans called to live at this important time, we can take our place in the dynamics of the evolutionary process; we can overcome autism and give expression to new human/Earth relations in their fullest form. In this shift from autism to literacy, liberation happens and hope is born. The shift from autism to literacy, from unconscious destruction to action for freedom is painful. We let go of, and die to, a consciousness of oppression in order to embrace liberation.

Moving Toward Liberation

As we bring to consciousness the obstacles to freedom that exist in our lives, and the desire we have to move toward greater fulfillment, we reflect on the following questions:

- From what idea, concept, hope, dream, or challenge do you feel held back?
- How do you see your consciousness of oppression affecting Earth?
- What have you done about this?
- What more do you need to know?
- What more needs to be done for Earth and its people?

Each of us is somewhere on the continuum between oppression and total freedom. When we present our experience and reflect on how we are held back, we are able to find our bearings and step off our great cultural treadmill. We are compelled to take action for freedom, to speak our words, and to fulfill our destinies. Audre Lourde once wrote: "Your silence will not protect you. It is not difference which immobilizes us but silence. And there are so many silences to be broken."

Each of us is called to break our silence, to speak our words of Earth literacy in a time when the moment is urgent and the outcome uncertain. Our challenge is to respond with new consciousness and unprecedented actions, to engage in a process of discovery that integrates thought and action in order to create a sustainable future. We see public life as a place of possibilities where we can say with Gandhi, "We must be the change we wish to see in the world." Our current culture is pathological, steeped in addictive behavior and misguided mysticism; consumerism and substance abuse distract us from our deeper purposes. Celebrating tomorrow means reinventing today. As we take up the challenge, we join with others to provide information and support to all those who are healing and liberating the people and the planet. As participants in a multicentered universe, we rediscover our place and our stories as part of the great cosmic unfolding. We give voice to what we most deeply believe and foster the leadership and resources necessary for all who would join us in this great adventure.

Earth literacy gives us new eyes: we see Earth in a new way. Then we take up the challenge of making the world different through dream, story, and action. I remember the story of the young couple who became separated in the snow drifts of Nevada. After days of doubt and struggle they miraculously found each other. In gratitude, they could say to each other through smiles and tears, "We would do anything for each other." When we extend this gesture to the entire Earth community, we have discovered the stuff of Earth literacy, the fabric for a mutually enhancing relationship between humans and Earth.

Reflection and Action for Cultural Genesis

FOR REFLECTION

Earth literacy expands the traditional meaning of the word literacy—to be Earth literate is to understand the basic languages "spoken" by Earth. It is to be knowledgeable with Earth's expertise as economist, educator, healer, law giver, and storyteller. You become aware at the deepest level of your consciousness that Earth's story is your story; you experience yourself in the unfolding drama of the universe. Earth literacy focuses on process, and story participation leads to a strong formational process aimed at healing our isolation from the natural world. It encourages inner and outer changes in a learner's consciousness, spirituality, values, and role choices.

—McGregor Smith[7]

We see the world not as a system that is simply in movement, but as one that is in a state of genesis.

—Pierre Teilhard de Chardin[8]

A vital goal ought to be "earth literacy" to foster both a scientific comprehension of the natural world and a broad-based environmental ethic of eco-justice. . . . It will require imagination and evocation as well as programs and practicality.

—Mary Evelyn Tucker[9]

You will learn more in the woods than you will in books. The trees and the stones will teach what you will never learn at the school of the masters.

—St. Bernard

We're here to learn the story and experience the dream.

—Thomas Berry

Action

1. Cultural historian Thomas Berry's life was profoundly transformed when as a small boy he experienced the "meadow across the creek" and realized that "nature was a thou' not an it'." This experience shaped and focused his life's work. Similarly, cosmologist Brian Swimme became enchanted by his early experience of the night sky. How has your life's work been shaped and formed by a primordial experience of Earth? Describe the ways this experience continues to influence you today.

2. Select a cultural form on which to reflect: education, spiritual psychology, justice, ecumenism, etc.

3. Use the principles of the universe (differentiation, subjectivity, and communion) to examine the form chosen. How are these principles honored? How are they ignored? How might they be more present? For example, in geo-justice, we examine local aspects (differentiation), psychosocial aspects (subjectivity) and global aspects (communion).

4. Create a *mandala* to express your insights. Accompany this image or picture by a descriptive statement (visual and literal media focus your reflection).

5. Through dialogue and reflection, select appropriate actions that will contribute to a renewed culture.

Although we can reflect and express ourselves as individuals, of course, the most fruitful action for cultural rebirth grows from group reflection and commitment, which is a practical example of the principle of communion out of diversity. If a group is not available for this process, I suggest that you keep a journal of your responses and, when possible, share them with one or more people.

FOR REFLECTION

1. How have your experiences with family, religion, education, and the bioregion of your childhood shaped and formed your perception of and relationship to the natural world?
2. What have you learned about yourself and Earth from these experiences?
3. Where are you in your journey regarding your relationship to the entire Earth community?

In the Beginning Was the Dream

— *The Dream*

Without a dream, the people perish.

—Proverbs 29:18

There is nothing like a dream
To create the future

—Victor Hugo

In the beginning was the dream
The dream was with the divine and the dream was divine.
The dream was with the divine in the beginning.
Through the dream all things come to be,
Not one thing had its being but through the dream.

—John 1:1–3 (paraphrased)

Earth literacy implies a cosmological awareness. It is a worldview that sees the human from the perspective of Earth. The inevitable unfolding of the universe does not give us reason to be passive witnesses of this cosmic process. We are not merely passengers on this evolutionary bus; rather, we are called to be passionate participants. Our role as humans at the threshold of a new millennium is to take initiative as agents of change. First, we must ask how we want our world to change. What will a renewed Earth be? What will a restructured society look like?

Our next step is to dream, for as humans in this process, it is important for us to know how we want this new culture to be before we move toward it. Every transformation is energized by a vision that takes us beyond our previous limits. The words of Robert Browning in *Andrea del Sarto* ring true here, "Ah, but a man's reach must exceed his grasp/ Or what's a heaven for?"

Our central problem as a culture and a people is that we have lost the dream. We must recapture our capacity to dream, to rekindle an experience of hope, to believe that tomorrow can be different from today. Only then can we overcome resignation, confusion, and despair. To dream is to summon the psychic energy and moral courage necessary to move into the future with responsibility and hope. It is to evoke a sacred and ecological vision that will foster and support enthusiasm for life. In fact, we have not only lost our dream, we have been conditioned by politicians and corporations to pursue the "American dream" of competition and conquest, a dream that is asynchronous with Earth and the Divine. As builders of a new culture we need to rediscover our personal, collective, and planetary dreams and attune them to a worldview based on diversity and interconnectedness.

In the United States, there has been a 45 percent rise in per capita consumption, with a 50 percent decrease in the quality of life. While ten million Americans own two or more homes, a minimum of 600,000 are homeless. As a country representing 5 percent of the planet's population, United States citizens consume 30 percent of Earth's goods. Within the lifetime of a child born today, virtually all of Earth's petroleum will be burned and Earth's fuel tank will be empty. While 78 percent of people are convinced something needs to be done to change the environment, only 22 percent are actually working to do something about it.

Additional concerns that evoke in us a feeling for the pain of human pathos and an experience of ecological bereavement include the following. Every two-thirds of a second a child dies of hunger. Forty million people die of hunger or hunger-related diseases each year. Seventeen thousand species become extinct each year. The ozone layer is so depleted in Australia that 99 percent of caucasians over the age of fifty will develop skin cancer. If all the water in the world were in a gallon jar, only one drop would be potable.

As we reflect on this overwhelming barrage of evidence for pathos and bereavement, we identify with the words of Vietnamese monk Thich Nath Hahn, who writes:

We hear within our hearts the sound of Earth—crying.

Yet, in our tears, we discover a reason to dream and the promise of a future filled with hope. No one has spoken more eloquently of this moment of fear and promise than a four-year-old child from Russia. These are her words:

May there always be sunlight.
May there always be trees.
May there always be mama and papa.
May there always be me.

Uncovering and reconnecting with our dreams enables us to confront the despair so deeply embedded in our cultural psyche. This eroded sense of worth envelops our collective soul as we face a growing number of problems brought on by structures of oppression, whether related to race, sex, class, or ecological devastation. One predictable result of our cultural cynicism and despair is *horizontal violence,* where the oppressed oppress one another: women discriminate against women; minorities undermine one another; and the poor oppress the poor. Injustice multiplies as the cycles accelerate. When we dream, we imagine how the world could be and take responsibility for bringing it about. When interest and imaginations are ignited by the dream, hope is possible. In the *mantra* of the Rainbow Coalition, we can keep hope alive. Our dreams make it possible for us to believe that tomorrow can be different from today. An inscription found on a church door in Essex, England gives voice to our hope:

A vision without a task is but a dream
A task without a vision is drudgery
A vision and a task is the joy of the world.

The challenge of cultural rebirth is to heal the chasm between our dream of how life could be and how it currently is. Implementing our dream will involve struggle and pain. We must want the dream badly enough to undergo the effort necessary to go beyond what seem to be our limits. Whether the obstructions are internal or external, we must not throw up our hands in the face of inevitable resistance to the new. In the face of our doubts and uncertainty, we are challenged to live our new dream, to put aside the operational doubt that follows upon our initial vision and rediscover a new "guiding star" that will energize our efforts and provide the courage and commitment to begin again. This process of beginning with a utopian vision as a resource for change is a constant in the lives of all who work to make a difference and become agents of transformation. It is also true that when we move toward putting our vision into practice, obstacles occur and doubt ensues. Thus, we must constantly reinvent the dream in the face of struggle and rediscover a new vision for our efforts as we strive again and again to reinvent our work. In this way, we constantly engage in efforts of resurrection, liberation, revolution and rebirth.

When the Rev. Martin Luther King, Jr., gave his last public speech in Memphis shortly before his assassination, he summarized the necessity and meaning of the dream of social equality. He spoke of no longer being afraid. He had "been to the mountain top." He had experienced a dream of how the world could be. Because of this, nothing could frighten him or hold him back. His dream of racial equality met incredible resistance from all sides. But his belief in his vision compelled him to work for its realization. His life challenges each of us to follow our dream and have its realization so fixed in our minds that nothing can hold us back. We need a vision of the future that is so real it gives us energy to act now.

At the age of sixteen, Natasha Dzura of Pennsylvania had a dream which movingly captures our collective vision of a future filled with hope.

> I have a dream that one day the children of the earth will frolic in a world of peace and harmony. That one day the people of every nation will take one another's hands and rise above pollution and destruction.
> I have a dream that one day Earth will feel safe resting softly upon our hands, knowing she will always remain cared for with us.
> I have a dream that the scars that have been inflicted upon her oceans, rainforests, and land will be healed by the loving hands of her children.
> I have a dream that all creation will be so delirious with joy that our voices will come together, all language and tones in a song of oneness. That we will dance on healed earth, swim in healed water, and breathe healed air.
> I have a dream that the creatures of every corner of Earth will come together and resurrect the planet, and I know that when this day comes we will be one with all things and find great joy in our happy, healthy mother, who will cradle us in her arms and give us a home for all eternity.[1]

What are our dreams? What common vision might we share? For some of us, our dream may be of an Earth where children are treasured, cities are safe, water runs pure, every member of every species is treated with integrity and love, and fear gives way to trust. The dream calls for action, as we strive to create a planet at peace.

> We all need a dream. Indeed, "without a dream the people perish." What is your dream? Stop here and reflect on what gives meaning to your life. Then present your dream in prose, poetry, art, or another medium. Post your representation where it will remind you of your true self and help counter the American dream that is pervasive in our culture. (My dream is included in the Appendix B of this book.)

The Prophetic Act

A major obstacle to fulfilling our dreams is that, historically, our spiritual traditions have not been at the service of transformation and change. There is often an implicit suggestion that spiritual practice and compassionate action are incompatible. Organized religion and the spirituality associated with it have often been on the side of the status quo. In Latin America, for example, there are two churches, the church of the people and the church of the regime. Too often, the religion of the regime has sanctioned oppression rather than confronted it.

Not only have we found it difficult to discover the resources for change in our spiritual traditions, but for the most part, the traditions of the mainline churches have been at the service of the status quo. The sanctioning of injustice by religion is highlighted by Billy Graham's presence at the White House the night before the United States engaged in military aggression against Iraq.

Our experience of being on the side of the oppressed calls us forward into a spirituality grounded in our traditions and yet boldly prophetic in the face of injustice and oppression. Dom Helder Camara counsels that we must carry a reverence for justice as a mother carries a reverence for her unborn child. It is this spirituality of reverence that will equip us to respond to the words of the Rev. Martin Luther King, Jr., who said, "Life's most persistent question is, What are we doing for others?"

As we make connections between spirituality and action, we see that our spirituality cannot be disembodied as it has been in the past. It cannot coexist with ecological devastation and social injustice. Rather, it summons us to solidarity and identification with the entire Earth community in a vision of harmony, balance, and peace. When we reflect on our experience from the perspective of the poor and Earth, we act differently. If we don't see the world through the eyes of the poor, we may tend to blame them. I remember driving through the barrios of Mexico City with a young man from the privileged class. He pointed to the poor people in their shanty town, saying they were poor because they were lazy. Similar comments are heard in reference to those on welfare or the homeless in our cities. When we see with their eyes, however, we cannot help but adopt a "preferential option for the poor," indeed, a preferential option for Earth.

As a new story of our origins (a new cosmology) and a renewed spirituality energize us for justice-making, our compassion is driven by the growing awareness that *everything* is intimately connected to everything else. We realize that each event or act of creation contains within itself the totality of creation.

Thomas Berry reminds us that our imaginations are most active when we dream. He invites us to see Earth as a result of the Divine imagination and challenges us to share the dream of Earth: "This awakening is our human participation in the dream of Earth, the dream that is carried in its integrity; not in any of Earth's cultural expressions, but in the depths of our genetic coding. Therein Earth functions at a depth beyond our capacity for active thought." Here, the dream is not some static goal to be clung to in a fixed way; rather the dream is the result of a fully imaginative and intuitive process that invites us into mystery and attunes our actions to the mind of the divine. In this way, the dream gives dynamism and direction to the future; it reveals archetypal forms emerging from the universe.

Thomas Berry compares the current state of the culture to a group of people who are together in a boat. Suddenly, a conflict erupts. As they wrangle, they notice the boat has sprung a leak. Aware that their common survival depends upon bailing out the boat, the passengers put aside their differences and collaborate on keeping their ship afloat.

This image of people moving from conflict to collaboration and survival reminds us that we need a dream big enough to dissolve discord, preserve the planet, and generate hope for the future.

Such a dream was dramatically portrayed when a teacher invited her students from a grade school in Manhattan to reflect through a drama on the current crisis and the need to dream of a healthy planet. In the play, one of the students played the part of Earth. As others in the play became aware that Earth was ill, they decided to perform surgery. During the surgery they removed the causes of the illness—aluminum cans, pesticides, styrofoam cups, plastics, poisoned water, unsorted garbage, and unrecycled bottles and papers. Aware after the surgery that Earth was still unable to return to full health, they began to provide her with clean water, pure air, and fresh soil. When these elements were received, Earth rose from her sick bed and began to dance joyfully with the children who restored her to full health. This truly is a dream that can carry us forward into the future, a dream of children playing happily on a healthy planet.

Dreams come alive when we realize the possibilities life presents. Tomorrow *can* be different from today, and cultural conflict and ecological devastation *can* be transformed into health and wholeness. Species *can* live together on this planet with respect and reverence for each other and their common home.

In classes and workshops, I am accustomed to engaging participants in the process of articulating their dreams through word and image. After reflecting on the crises and opportunities of our times, I invite them to complete this sentence: *I have a dream. . . .* When they have completed this exercise, I present the participants with a number of different colored balls of yarn. As they stand in a circle and throw balls of yarn back and forth, a multicolored tapestry forms, a symbol of diversity and connectedness. Then after proclaiming their dream to the group they are invited to toss the papers containing their dreams onto the yarn, which functions as a vast dream catcher. I have learned through this process that our dream of the future will be motivated by images of beauty and grace; in our dreaming, we summon the courage to question our assumptions about life, to allow our current perceptions to be "shattered," and to move toward the future in yet unprecedented ways.

To dream of a future yet unformed requires that we be liberated from patterns of conformity and predictable behavior. The example of a fish in a tank divided by a partition illustrates this. When the partition is removed, the fish continues to swim within its previous confines, although it could now move through the whole tank. Our behaviors, too, can be limited by habit and perception. We need to ask ourselves about the false perceptions and partitions in our lives and face the challenge to find new frontiers and patterns of behavior.

Let us return for a moment to Thomas Berry's image of people in a boat. Berry presents three options as we face the crisis of the leaking boat of ecological bereavement: (1) we can have tantrums and continue to act out our aggression on Earth; (2) we can fall back upon ourselves and jump out of the boat to our deaths, culturally and ecologically; or (3) we can turn around, bail out the boat, row forward, and begin again. With the courage to make our dreams big enough, we can begin again, bail out the boat of ecological devastation, depart from ingrained patterns of conformity, change our perception of the planet, and realize the dream of healthy people on a flourishing planet.

Energized by our dreams, we tell stories as one step toward action and liberation. We return again to the realization that the dream is the origin point that resides within the divine imagination that culminates in the re-creation of Earth and all its species. To paraphrase John 1:1–3 yet another way:

> In the beginning was the dream,
> And the dream was with us
> Erupting from the heart of the universe and the mind of the Divine
> Discovering self-expression
> Within the contours of plants, animals, and people
> Emerging from the recesses of life.

FOR REFLECTION

The dream drives the action.

—Carl Jung

Hope is a state of mind, not of the world. Hope, in this deep and powerful sense, is not the same as joy that things are going well, or willingness to invest in enterprises that are obviously heading for success, but rather an ability to work for something because it is good, not because it stands for a chance to succeed.

—Vaclav Havel

The future belongs to those who give the next generation reason for hope.

—Pierre Teilhard de Chardin

Just as the ruined landscapes we see about us are the visible dreams of the past, so any future world restored in its primordial loveliness must first come into being in the dreams that arise from the primordial depths within us. Without such dreams none of our efforts at purifying this toxic planet or establishing a viable mode of existence of the Earth will succeed.

—Thomas Berry

The dream is at the heart of the action.

—Thomas Berry

If you go back to your earliest dreams as a child, some of the answers will be there. Our greatest energy comes from our dreams and visions. So may you find that wellspring and find the spirit speaking clearly.

—Miriam MacGillis[2]

How do the ways I live and the choices I make affect the realization of my dream for Earth? Remember the dreams of your childhood! Write them, paint them, reflect on them that they may energize and activate your life.

Complete this statement: "I have a dream . . ."

Unfolding Mystery and Meaning
— The Story

We explain things by telling their story—how they came into being and the changes that have taken place over the course of time . . . whether minutes or millennia. . . . This is especially true in explaining those profound formative influences that have shaped our sense of the sacred.

—Thomas Berry[1]

Listening and Recognition

A student once asked me how I had arrived at my present understanding of spirituality, justice, and Earth. I realized that the best answer lay in my family story. Memories of my father came into sharper focus when a group of men gathered at a California ranch to examine our relationships with our fathers. We told many stories that weekend. As the others did, I knew my father—and myself—better when I returned home. Our storytelling had deepened our awareness, and, for some, healing had come in our remembering and telling.

My father was a young boy when his mother died, leaving him with his two sisters and brothers. He was a man of superior intelligence who regretfully received only a sixth grade education. He did factory work in the Detroit automotive industry during the winter and farmed the ungiving clay of Canada's southwestern Ontario in the summer. During the Great Depression, he worked for twenty-five cents an hour and endured the hopeful stares of the unemployed, who waited at the roadside to see whether he would succumb to the weight of his burden and drop his shovel. I remembered the bittersweet time the two of us lived together after my mother died. I remembered my dad attending our baseball games when my brother and I were growing up. I remembered his joy at being a grandfather when my brother's first child was born. And I painfully recalled his last afternoon. We went for a Sunday drive, not knowing that later that evening he would die in his sleep.

The circumstances of my early years have been influential in my life's journey as well. As a result of my mother's illness, I spent the first four and one-half years of my life with her two sisters. I was loved and well cared for, but I was also on the margin of my family. I came to feel that I existed between two worlds, two homes. One home was that of my parents, brother, and sister; the other was that of my aunts. This displacement has had two major influences. One is a deep longing for a home, which has resulted in a passionate interest in ecology and geo-justice, the search for a home here on planet Earth. The other is my struggle to be connected, often to major institutions, at the same time that I move away from the centers, whether they be religious, academic, or political. It seems to me that the edge is where liberation is possible.

The potato famine that so deeply devastated my Irish ancestors also has had a profound effect on how I feel about the poor. My sister, Mary, was interviewed by the *Asbury Park Press* regarding her work with the local food bank in New Jersey. When asked why she was doing this volunteer work, her reply was, "My ancestors suffered from the potato famine." When I heard this, I realized it was true for me, too, and I began to ask myself about the reasons behind my passionate interest in geo-justice.

Somehow, I have always felt a deep desire to assist people in discovering what they most deeply want for their lives. This is accompanied by a conviction that when people achieve their own deepest desires, the results will be just. At the same time, as I examine my life, I realize that this impulse toward justice-making is a combination of many emotions— vulnerability, desire, outrage, pain, aspiration, struggle, and hope. Geo-justice draws me forward for many reasons—deep-seated anger, an experience of alienation and being an outsider, and a vision of a better world for all children. My attraction to geo-justice is a mix of many factors, some noble, others the result of my wounds. As I have researched my own story, I have come to know where the energy and commitment for geo-justice have their genesis.

In the early seventies, I met Monsignor Jack Egan and became the Canadian liaison to the Board of the Catholic Committee on Urban Ministry. Later I became the chairperson for Catholics for Social Change in Canada. I had found a home, a place on the edge among these church-related people concerned about peace, justice, and civil rights. We formed a people, a church, who, during the Vietnam war and the movement led by the Rev. Martin Luther King, Jr., worked to build the city of God in a country torn by riots, protests, and confusion. I felt connected to these men and women. We were on the edge of the church, but we were at the center of the issues that rocked the continent and, more important, touched the lives of people.

Thinking about my Canadian roots, I realize that my homeland was born out of colonialism and a connection to the crown; alternatively, the United States became a republic through revolution. The diverse origins of these two countries profoundly affects the psyches of their people and their response to the urgent concerns of our times. During the Vietnam war, Canada became a haven for American exiles whose consciences put them in conflict with their government's foreign policy. But, despite its espousal of multiculturalism, Canada has not been exempt from racial strife, although it is true that Canada was not affected as deeply by the Civil Rights Movement. On the other hand, the cultural crises of the United States have reminded Canadians of the need to heal the wounds between Quebec and the rest of the country as well as to re-examine our relationship to the indigenous peoples of our own land.

As I reflected on my story, I began to understand that my story is also the story of a people who wanted for their country what they believed God wanted for both people and planet. This narrative of my journey, our journey, has revealed much to me about the power of story. Our story truly discloses who we are and, more important, who we can become.

The Unfolding Story

"Fifteen billion years after the fireball foamed into existence, five billion years after Earth arrived on the scene, this new form of existence enabled the powers of the universe to carry forth within conscious self-awareness. Through the emergence of the human, the universe folded back on itself and gathered its power onto a new form for the beginning of the next great era of its unfolding story."[2]

The unfolding story in its elegance and simplicity evokes a primordial interrelatedness. Convinced that we are deeply connected in a common origin and a shared destiny, and knowing that our lives are profoundly congruent with the events of the universe, we experience deep joy. Our story reminds us that the relationships we achieve with humans and the natural world are activated by intimacy and fostered by love. Enveloped in the narrative of the great story, we experience belonging and awaken to the powers of mystery, the Divine Source of all that is. Life becomes a place of possibility, where human pathos and ecological bereavement can be transformed with the promise of grandeur and stunning beauty. As cosmologist Timothy Ferris says of the universe: "Its story is our story, too." Theologian Elizabeth Johnson writes, "The kinship model of humankind's relation to the natural world is not just a poetic, good-hearted way of seeing things, but the basic truth."

The sequence of transformational events—the galactic story, Earth story, life story, and human story—continually reminds us that we are all made from stardust. The atoms of our bodies are formed from the stars. It is here that life happens and energy is transformed. All of us are privileged to listen to and tell the cosmic story. We understand the story through science, ingest it through spiritual practice, and express it in various creative forms. The story reveals that Earth is not fatally flawed; rather, the story tells us that in the crisis of our time, we must discover a new way of seeing and living in the world. Our task is not to transcend the universe, but to enter it.

Stories let us look back and learn and then look forward and act differently. Stories are about what is done or not done, said or not said; they capture our energies, startle us, and stay with us. Stories name what is important; they save us from the linearity of the "little boxes" of our lives. They provide patterns of coherence and unity. Stories carry meaning, history, and purpose, and they recount moments of love, insight, appreciation, and loss. Stories also enhance commitment, release power for living, and make us more attentive to the sacredness of life, the beauty of the natural world, and the basis of our belief.

Stories move us deeply as they teach, inform, and transform. Stories return us to our origins and invite us into mystery. Stories reveal what is sacred and connect us through symbol and image to the ultimate questions of meaning, purpose, and our relationship to the divine. Stories remind us of where we come from, of our roots and our ancestors; they invite us to see the universe acting through us.

We know others better when they tell us their stories, and we know ourselves better when we reflect on and share our own stories. As we disclose our identity and roots, our stories contribute to comprehension and acceptance, deepen our relationships, and create communion and continuity as we reflect on the turning points of our lives.

I have learned that, for me, storytelling is the best way to teach, learn, and communicate. When we tell stories, as we did in the men's group, we generate themes from our narratives and are better able to interpret our experience. Theology happens through storytelling when we connect our story to the story of our tradition. When we hear the story of Earth as a communication from the Divine, we deepen the meaning of our life.

When we tell our stories of oppression and share our dreams, we begin to move into action that will be liberating and free. Stories reconstruct our consciousness, confirm our deeper knowing, and challenge us to go beyond the dream to action. In the healing process, we go back to the beginning and begin again; through action, we heal our story and begin to create a new one.

When we see our individual story and our cultural story within the larger context of Earth story and the universe story, we quench our thirst for meaning and discover the context for all stories. We overcome alienation and reorient our consciousness toward a more integral relationship with Earth.

Geo-justice: A Preferential Option for Earth

As the years have passed, I have revised my approach to justice-making. I have striven to bring it into alignment with the new story I hear emerging from science, art, and spiritual practice. I understand now that the creation-centered paradigm of the paschal mystery (incarnation, crucifixion, and resurrection) and Pentecost is also the dynamic of our journey into justice-making in and through Earth. By applying this to Earth, I see profound implications for geo-justice. I see the connections between justice for all creation and the work of Saul Alinsky, Paulo Freire, and others (outlined later in this book). The results of my reflections have combined the dynamics of change with the concepts of Earth in what I now call geo-justice. This is my way of telling the story of geo-justice.

We stand at a crossroads of momentous proportions. This profound moment of crisis and transition calls us to passionate action for social and environmental justice; we need to liberate Earth and its peoples.

Geo-justice is about living within and attuned to the natural world; as we become one with the universe, we are healed of any divisions and experience the joy of living in harmony with all that is.

Geo-justice is a dramatic re-enactment of the paschal mystery (life, death, and resurrection) located within Earth dynamics of loss and return; it is always a work of the heart, bringing about inspiration and hope, inviting our participation as we fashion a fabric of compassion.

Even as Earth is in danger of becoming a wasteland, we are challenged to put our energies where there is potential for life, to bring about new structures, new stories, and new forms as we move from the dark night of our cultural soul to wellsprings of hope. As we die to alienation and addiction in its many forms, we rise to balance and connectedness, we "make our Easter with Earth."

Geo-justice weaves together the global, local, and psychosocial components as we fashion language and images for our common work. We awaken from the dream of separateness, tell our stories, relate to the particular place on the planet where we live (our bioregion), and remember our relationship to the land. We discover that the way to the sacred is through the place of our dwelling. We come to understand Earth's oppression as our own. As we embrace the interior life and the world around us as one, we strive to heal the fragmentation within and the alienation without.

We celebrate the energy of interconnectedness within the psyche and our political and social systems through a descent into the deeper understanding and experience of relatedness; it is thus that "we heal what is broken, reunite what is separate, and recreate the face of Earth."[3] Planetary Pentecost becomes a work of the heart to heal pain and liberate Earth and its peoples. It is a response to the sacred impulse and a deep knowing that we are "as much Earth as rocks, water and trees".[4] Geo-justice is our work for today grounded in our vision for tomorrow.

As I examined more fully the meaning of story and its implications for our lives, I began to understand more fully the content of the story that the universe and Earth communicate to us. I now understand that the story reveals the three basic principles that are present in the universe: differentiation, interiority, and communion. When these principles are present, the relationship between people and planet achieves its deepest purpose, and the Divine is present in our midst. When these principles are coded into the culture, then harmony, balance, and peace are present, and geo-justice becomes manifest among us.

Each of us is a unique manifestation of the Divine, with our particular gifts and responsibilities. We also have received the capacity to experience mystery and give expression to the voice that lies within. Together, we are bonded into a pattern of relationships, the "curvature of compassion" that embraces the entire Earth. These patterns and dynamics find their source and reflection in the Trinity, a divine community of equality and diversity. Thus, we see that the Creator is the source of uniqueness and diversity; the Word provides the source of meaning, purpose, depth, and story; and the Spirit is the source of relatedness and interconnection. The Trinity is the culmination of the cosmic story, the new creation.

To embody fully these patterns of the universe is to live out the commandments of creation and to be true to the ethics of each tradition, to achieve and realize a global ethos. When differentiation, interiority, and communion are present in our culture, the culture is reborn, geo-justice emerges, and the Divine is palpable and present in our midst.

When we see our individual story and our cultural story within the larger context of Earth story, we quench our thirsts for meaning and discover the context for all our stories. We overcome alienation and reorient our consciousness toward a more integral relationship with Earth.

The words of Meister Eckhart encourage us on our journey. He writes, "Become aware of what is in you. Announce it, pronounce it, produce it, and give birth to it."[5] The following is my own articulation of the implications of the principles of the universe in cultural form—a further expression of geo-justice.

Creativity and Uniqueness

The sacred impulse to give birth and pass something on is at the heart of the creative process. Some things we do because we feel we have to leave something behind. In the struggle that creativity involves, we surrender to the outcome without knowing what will happen. We remain open as the process unfolds. Just as the seed is never still present when the tree grows, creativity, too, is about resurrection. Something new is born in the continual unfolding dynamic of life. The process of death and return is deeply woven into the fabric of life; harmony with Earth in its life–death–life cycle is preferable to domination and control. The results of our creativity have a life of their own and often surprise us.

At the heart of creativity is diversity. Diversity is at the core of the universe and is its art form. We need to embrace and appreciate the differences in places and people. However, creativity and diversity have not been espoused by the bureaucratic structures of our dominant culture. Schools, governments, and corporations prefer predictable, managed behavior. In the creative process, we surrender and often become astonished at what happens as we revere the diversity of ethos, language, history, and place. As we challenge the conformity that leads to boredom and burnout, the door opens to joy, inspiration, and healing. As we participate in any particular manifestation of beauty, we contribute to the epiphany that expresses the divine manifestation of mystery that engages us more fully in the rapture and surprise that life is. All of this, of course, may be perceived as threat—or craziness—by the established structures.

Our creativity is not about comparison or competition. It is the incarnational energy finding expression in our imaginations and lives as we choose what we really want to create. In this process, we create the creator as well as the work of art; that is, as we paint a picture, we simultaneously transform the landscape of our soul and ourselves become new.

Creativity also happens in the psyche when our consciousness shifts from being human-centered to being creation-centered. Creativity rescues us from a preoccupation with being healed and deepens our appreciation of beauty and blessing. It is thus that we are healed from a fragmentation within and an alienation without. Creativity is knowing and trusting the images that emerge from within; it is the radical and revolutionary art of swimming in the current of life. We trust our images, go beyond the self, and awaken to the divine presence that finds expression through us.

Interiority and Depth

Each of us is motivated by a desire to have access to our inner depths, those reservoirs of inexhaustible energy and experience. Awakening to our interior sensitivities helps us to experience more fully the beauty, mystery, darkness, and recesses of human self-awareness and the dynamic balance of Earth.

To become artists of geo-justice, we must make conscious the story that is operative in our lives. When we connect to these deep places within, we touch the footprints of God in our lives. Our interior realm is a place of incredible vastness when viewed from the perspective of the cosmos rather than the confines of human experience. Our lives are nourished by the beauty of the cosmos and Earth; we ingest and make the mystery of creation part of our lives as we celebrate and welcome the galactic constellations and depths of our interior experience. We incarnate life's mysteries and listen from inside to the voice that speaks to us through the seas, sky, and trees.

Within our interior existence, we contact God, gain access to the Word, and become new people of a new Earth. From this perspective, we design and demonstrate through ritual, art, and story the congruence between our vision and our action. Through silence, movement, art, metaphor, image, and music we create rituals of empowerment. As we utilize ancient forms, we celebrate both what is signified and brought about in the culture. Our imaginations expand, and we face the future with hope, peace, and purpose.

Communion and Compassion

Justice-making as a preferential option for the poor is a major contribution of liberation theology. When this is extended to Earth, we have discovered a new meaning of poverty.

Many are troubled by the pain of social and ecological injustice as well as the approaches taken in attempting to heal this injustice. We need to discover more and better ways to support our efforts to liberate the oppressed. We need to see justice-making as an adventure in communion rather than an experience of fragmentation and alienation, an experience that is exciting and empowering, involving both revolution (structural change) and reformation (internal change). The conviction that we need to liberate the oppressor as well as the oppressed in our organizing for justice is an important component of the process.

The comprehensive bonding and compassionate embrace that brings everything in the universe into relationship with everything else reflects the reality that relationship is the essence of existence and the central dynamic of compassion. As we courageously open our hearts to the pain of the planet, we participate in expressing and experiencing the healing properties of Earth. From this perspective, justice-making extends itself to embrace the entire natural world. Earth itself becomes an archetype for our justice-making.

Communion and compassion are central to life; they are stories of relationship and connectedness. We can adopt as our theme the words of Meister Eckhart: "Those who follow compassion find life for themselves, justice for their neighbor, and glory for God."[6]

When we see that Earth is a living, interconnected system with the properties of self-healing, harmony, and peace, we are invited to participate in a communion of relationships through which we experience and express compassion as our agenda for today and our hope for tomorrow. As we connect to the poor of Guatemala and to the rainforest of Brazil, we fashion a web of compassion that extends our relationships to both the atmosphere and the street. When we are moved to compassion toward people and the natural world, we treat both with a reverence and love that is intimate, fully vulnerable, and connected.

The Rebirth of Culture

As we stand at the doorway of a new culture, we see that the incarnation is, indeed, a continuous event. "Bethlehem" is our home today. Earth, and time are sacramental and interconnected.

The rebirth of culture will generate and be formed by new stories and myths. The specific tendencies of these stories will be influenced by our own stories, so that we can live in a more healing manner on the planet as the Divine breaks through and becomes incarnate in diverse ways.

In the rebirth of culture, we strive for hope and awareness—often in the face of resignation and silence—so that we may face the future with a vision, a story fashioned from a constellation of relationships that is fresh and transformed.

As we become aware of where people hurt and where devastation takes place, we also discover where liberation can happen and foster the flame of hope. Through the continuing incarnation, the rebirth of culture continues to happen among us.

The Power of Story for Liberation

When we come together and tell the stories of our relationships to ancestors and Earth, memories are activated, energy is released, and action follows. Storytelling is the most radical act of organizing. It provides the energy and direction for collective action. When we tell the story of the universe and Earth, and see our own stories in the context of these larger stories, the action that follows will be in harmony with Earth and all its species.

In meeting rooms and church basements across the continent, people are gathering to tell their stories of hope for better schools, safer neighborhoods, and green space for their children. Some stories evoke moral outrage and release prophetic action. The Pacific Institute for Community Organization with John Bauman in Oakland, California, the Brooklyn Ecumenical Cooperatives, and the Portland Organizing Project in Oregon with Richard Harmon, are important projects that channel the energy of stories into justice-making. Harmon says, "When we sit with each other in our church basements or across our kitchen tables, we know how important our storytelling and future imaging really is. We come to understand that, yes, we are speaking from the center of our sacredness. We come to understand that Earth, in its choking pain and tenderness, is speaking through us."[7]

These words name the context and focus of storytelling in community settings across the country. When we ask, "What was the basic struggle for each generation?" and "What did each generation do about it?" they begin to realize that family roots reach deep into the past and, that our ancestors struggled with values and conflicts about the land. In our stories, the past becomes alive and present; divine energy becomes operative in our midst. Our engagement gives birth to a renewed vision that will be realized from our energies and our stories. In storytelling, we retrieve our past as we mold our future.

The story of Nelson Mandela and the African National Congress was generated from years of apartheid, imprisonment, and pain. This maturation of a people into democratic self-determination grew out of the stories of the people of Soweto and other townships—places where people gathered with the courage to name and respond to the oppression of institutionalized racism. Their response has led to a revolution of hope and the beginnings of a government based on full participation.

Stories of oppression and hope also have provided the energy to build a church in Latin America. Through naming the alliance of the institutional church with the military regimes, a people's church has emerged.

I know that when I reflect on my life, when I tell my story, I feel refreshed and motivated. Stories heal our soul and piece together a quilt of hope. Our reflection on our story and Earth's story reminds us of the story of our core tradition and roots. In this remembering, we discover hope and peace. Through story, we discover meaning and experience being truly alive. Our imagination is graced and erupts into a renewed vision of geo-justice, peace, and freedom. In our stories, we recover our dreams, remember the young of every species, and acquire energy for action. After all, the children are counting on us.

FOR REFLECTION

The great story of the universe, the story of Earth, and the story of the human have seemed too distant from each other to be encompassed within a single presentation. Now, however, the urgency is such that we can no longer isolate these various components of Earth from each other. This urgency includes all these elements of the great story, but especially the story of Earth: its difference from the other planets; its primordial shaping; the emergence of life in the seas and on the land in all their varieties and their interdependence; the diversity in bioregional life communities from the arctic tundra to the tropical rainforests, from the high mountain communities to the coastal regions.

—Thomas Berry[8]

I hope you will go out and let stories happen to you and that you will work them; water them with blood and tears and your laughter till they bloom, till you yourself burst into bloom.

—Clarissa Pinkola Estes[9]

A Process for Stories

1. With one or two others, look back over three or four generations. For each generation ask two questions:
    What was the basic value for this generation?
    What did this generation do about the land?
    Practice listening and recognition with tenderness and determination as you explore common themes that result from this process.
2. Be sure to name some "epiphanies" and "successes" in the efforts of your own or previous generations.
3. At the end, allow time to reflect on this experience of deep sharing and remembering your roots. What relationships were fostered and what actions will result from this process?

The Cosmic Walk

Prepare a calibrated rope marked according to the events named below. Place the rope in a spiral starting from the center of the room. Place a candle and a placard naming each event. In turn, participants step into the spiral, light a candle by the placard and proclaim the event. When all candles are lit, each person steps into the spiral and moves from the center outward, observing the events of the universe. When the participants exit the spiral, they declare, "The universe celebrates (name)" and are welcomed by the group. This ritual was developed by Sr. Miriam Therese McGillis of Genesis Farm.

The New Story

15 billion years ago	The universe came into being
5 billion years ago	The solar system and Earth emerged
3 billion years ago	Life emerged as simple bacteria

2 billion years ago	Oxygen formed in the atmosphere
1 billion years ago	Earth reproduced life sexually
800 million years ago	Multicellular life emerged
520 million years ago	The first fish emerged
420 million years ago	The first land plants appeared
360 million years ago	The first insects came to be
220 million years ago	The first mammals emerged
180 million years ago	The first birds took flight
130 million years ago	The first flowering plants appeared
65 million years ago	Dinosaurs became extinct
5 million years ago	The Ice Age occurred
100 thousand years ago	*Homo sapiens* emerged
10 thousand years ago	Agriculture began
7 thousand years ago	Abraham and Sarah left Ur
2 thousand years ago	Jesus of Nazareth was born
1 hundred years ago	The first photograph was created
57 years ago	The atom was split
28 years ago	The first human stepped on the moon
7 years ago	The wall between East and West disintegrated
Today	The universe dreams us forth by name

Fueling Our Acts of Re-Creation
— *The Action*

They're oppressed by taxation and inflation, poisoned by pollution, terrorized by urban crime, frightened by the new youth culture, baffled by the computerized world around them. They've worked all their lives to get their own little house in the suburbs, their color TV, their two cars, and now the good life seems to have turned to ashes in their mouths. Their personal lives are generally unfulfilling, their jobs unsatisfying; they've succumbed to tranquilizers and pep pills; they drown their sorrows in alcohol; they feel trapped in long-term endurance marriages, or escape into guilt-ridden divorces. They're depersonalized, without any feeling in the political process, and they feel rejected and hopeless. Their Utopia of status and security has become a ticky–tacky suburb; their splitlevels have sprouted prison bars, and their disillusionment has become terminal. . . .

When they turn on the TV and the news comes on, they see the almost unbelievable hypocrisy and deceit and often outright idiocy of our national leaders and the corruption and disintegration of all our institutions, from the police and courts to the White House itself. Their society seems to be crumbling, and they see themselves as no more than small failures within a larger failure. All their values seem to have deserted them, leaving them rudderless in a sea of social chaos.

—Saul Alinsky[1]

May the Future Happen Now

We must put vision into action. . . . If we want to live healthy lives, we have to build into our daily life moments of vision and then let our action be formed by that vision.

—David Steindl-Rast, OSB

We stand at the precipice of a new millennium, confronted with the reality of a deep paradox: things are coming to an end yet beginning. Today is marked by a fusion of doom and hope, destruction and newness.

We anticipate tomorrow as a social and ecological utopia, yet we remain enveloped in "the twentieth-century blues."

Our cultural soul is trapped in a fixation that the world is coming to an end. Conservative groups promote an Armageddon mentality that looks forward to the rapture of being close to God at the end-time. The Branch Davidians of Waco, Texas, and the terrorists of Oklahoma City are classic examples of the madness of our historical moment. In addition, a distorted vision of the materialist *mantra* "more is better" has weakened our actions for the poor, oppressed, and disadvantaged. Faced with these reactionary distortions, we are called to tell again our stories of struggle, those narratives that recover an awareness of the intrinsic worth of all creation. With moral clarity and political strength, we move into action, with our initiatives nourished by a new appreciation of science.

My mind goes back to a class in the philosophy of science, which I attended as an undergraduate at Assumption University of Windsor (now the University of Windsor). I began to realize then that science and religion can be complementary sources for a common truth. As St. Thomas Aquinas asserted, there are two sources of revelation: The Book of Scripture and the Book of Nature. I celebrated the affirmation of Pope Pius XII regarding the wisdom and truth contained in the insights and postulates of an expanding and evolving universe. As a chemistry major, I felt comforted to know that there was a coherence between the tenets of my tradition and the new discoveries being developed through science.

Moreover, I began to realize that science and religion needed to move beyond conflict and independence toward increased levels of dialogue and integration. I began to understand God's action in the world from the perspective of the Exodus and the paschal mystery; the divine presence became palpable to me as I reflected on the words of Mechtild of Magdeburg: "The day of my spiritual awakening I saw and knew that I saw God in all things and all things in God."

Through this experience of panentheism, I gained a greater insight into mystery. I realized that I was as much in God as the fish is in water. Concurrently, I began to realize that there is a seamless garment between the social and the ecological, between culture and nature. I also began to grasp more fully the drama of life and to understand God's action in the world. Suddenly, the mystery began to make sense; I could feel creation pulsing in and through every aspect of existence. Science and spirituality had become friends; I now understood the principles of an expanding and evolving universe as God's action in the world. These two great sources of wisdom had become complementary places where action happens, and all creation can be healed and made whole again.

It is action that fuels and focuses our efforts; it takes us outside ourselves and fosters self-discovery. When properly planned and practiced, action tests our values, develops leaders, and achieves results. The movement into action through literacy, dream, and story takes place in various ways. I propose that organizing, education, psychology, deep ecology, and economics can be vehicles of action that can culminate in the common effort I call a Coalition for Earth.

Actions are generated by dreams and storytelling; they bubble up from within, build bridges to others, and culminate in resolution and hope. Actions return us to our origins; we remember the struggle of our ancestors and move forward with renewed energy and hope. Actions are based on trust, courage, and letting go of predictable results. Actions transcend pitfalls and pressures; they give voice to our dreams and provide a means for realizing from our stories of grief, pain, and hope an experience of health and wholeness.

In our movement from action to liberation, we realize that everything is revelatory and related; each of us with our gifts and difficulties is moved by awe and a commitment to contribute to a new cultural coding that is congruent with the activities of the of the universe. Our liberation involves the shattering of previous perceptions and the determination to move forward in new and unprecedented ways; new ways that celebrate mystery and meaning, while simultaneously seizing the opportunity to remake the world.

Organizing: The First Act of Justice-Making

"The silence of the stars is the silence of creation and re-creation."
—Chet Raymo

The phrase *middle class,* as described by Saul Alinsky, names my experience and, I would suggest, the experience of most of you who are reading these pages. We hold a place of ambiguity and ambivalence in society. We are oppressed by those who occupy a higher economic bracket, and we feel the demands of those less privileged. Yet, we are the people who must act if our society is to be restructured and our Earth restored. The challenge is ours; to accept it, we must join hands with the less privileged, with those who have no voice in our society. Together we can create the critical mass of energy necessary to bring about the change for which the poor and Earth are crying. Having labored in institutions—academic, ecclesiastic, and public—I have witnessed the incredibly deadening results when a people's energy is co-opted by an institutional agenda. This happens so frequently that we scarcely notice. The best of intentions, the greatest of generosity, become blunted and diluted as we lose touch with our deepest aspirations and fondest hopes. However, I have also seen and experienced the rewards of inspiration and hope that flow when we are involved in organizational efforts energized by our passions. The challenge is to distill from the diverse approaches to change and organization the universal principles that are designed to bring about justice. *Organize* is a verb that names the constellation of relationships that make spontaneity possible and geo-justice a realizable goal.

The organizing process mediates the discontinuity between our dream and our acts. Organization involves a reintegration of the human process within Earth process. We see ourselves of and within Earth. Our actions for change become acts of co-creativity, and we work together in realizing the dream through the organizing process.

There is currently a renaissance of organizing in our culture, frozen as it is by the shock of rapid change. One outcome of organizing will be the development of mediating structures that connect contemporary culture to the evolving Earth community. These structures are emerging as a result of engaging the strategy of literacy, dream, and story.

In storytelling, we tell their story and Earth story. The resultant action demonstrates that organization is indeed about story in action. It's about our story lived out in the context of the universe. It is through continuing to gather and tell stories that actions steps are revealed.

Community Organization

In a Chicago classroom, I listened to Saul Alinsky lecture on community organization, an area in which he became the acknowledged architect and leader. I asked then, as I do now, about the meaning of his radical vision, a vision that fueled a movement "to do something practical to help the poor, the hungry, the imprisoned and the powerless." What are the implications of Alinsky's work?

I've come to realize that community organization is a powerful vehicle for transformation and change. The organizing process brings hope, courage, and creativity to people afflicted by malignant inertia and mass resignation. The organizing process challenges us to think on our feet and reflect on life in a disciplined way. To organize effectively is to be both fixed and fluid in our approach—one foot solidly on the ground and the other moving. Through action and reflection, the organizer creates a synthesis that leads to an ever more informed action.

Primarily, organizing is about communication, relationship, and the capacity to listen. Through this interconnectedness, we become more sensitive to the central interests of others. The organizing process involves developing strategies and tactics that respond to those interests. To organize is not to memorize a set of tactics to be repeated in a particular context; rather, it is to become politically competent and attuned to a set of universal principles whose particular application will grow out of the particular circumstance of the people. Tacticians of transformation have always resisted articulating strategies lest they be repeated by others and not recreated in the new context. For example on one occasion Alinsky, when negotiating for change on a college campus employed as a tactic the placing of large wads of bubble gum on the walkways; the result was that it became difficult to move about the campus. This highlighted the greater issue of blocked communications at the college. Unfortunately many began to immitate this approach although in different settings; as a result, it had little meaning.

The organizer achieves satisfaction from the effectiveness of the people. To remain fresh and effective, the organizing process must be continually regenerated and renewed. Historically if it is not, after five to eight years, an organization will oppose the original purpose for which it was developed!

The organizer has a profound belief in people and a deep trust that, when properly informed, they will act justly. A characteristic of the organizer is the capacity to find a positive in every negative, although organizing, like life, has peaks and valleys—its dramatic intervals and its tedious and monotonous moments. Always motivated by the desire for equality, freedom, and peace, the organizing process enhances solidarity and increases our ability to act. The organizer and the organizing process are fueled by curiosity and trust. The effectiveness of the organizing process hinges on finding and training leaders who, through life experience, intelligence, and other qualities, can move to the forefront in any organizational effort.

Organizing is the first act of justice-making. It enables us to do together what we could not accomplish alone. Organizing is not so much about doing things for others as it is about creating the possibilities for people to do things for themselves. The classic example is that of either giving a hungry person a fish, or organizing to provide a fishing pole so the hungry person has the means to obtain food.

The organizing process occurs in four phases: preorganizing, disorganizing, organizing, and reorganizing. The preorganizing phase involves establishing relationships with individuals and groups in the community. This must be done carefully. The goal is not to create conflict or friction, but to elevate hope and possibility.

Disorganizing shakes things up. By bringing groups previously unrelated to the patterns of power into relationship with the community, for example, forces that previously opposed people's interests are dissolved.

Organizing involves creating new organizational units around issues; it also means regenerating older or inactive groups. This is when we consider how to develop the new structures needed for the organization we want to build. Reorganizing brings new and previously existing structures together through immediate, specific, realizable, and winning actions.

The Preorganizing Phase

This is the stage at which the organizer moves into the community. The intention is to build trust and listen to what the people have to say without taking sides. The result of this process is to elevate the sense of hope and possibility among the people. They see themselves with increased dignity and value and begin to believe that they can accomplish something with their lives.

The preorganizing phase is very much about dream and vision. In approaching a community, Alinsky stood valiantly on the side of dignity and self-respect. He supported people's "desperate search for identity,"[2] which he deeply believed could be realized through participation in organization. "Change comes from power; power comes from organization, an approach that builds hope in the idea of organization and in people themselves."[3] It was because of his association with Saul Alinsky that Msgr. John Egan could say, "The first act of social justice is organization."[4]

Community organization, as designed and taught by Alinsky and his colleagues, brought new meaning into my life. As I wrote in a reflection at the time:

> I find this stuff so exciting. It seems for years I've been working through and with structures that militate against liberating people and serving them. The whole thing that turns me on about community organization is that it provides a vehicle whereby most people can move and struggle out of their own passions and interest in life.[5]

This conviction, shared by so many others, was my response to the vision and passion with which Alinsky approached his work. For Alinsky, organization provided the entry into people's greatest question: Why am I here?

It is in light of this curiosity, which is so deep in all of us, that he quoted scientist Niels Bohr: "Every sentence I utter must be understood, not as an affirmation, but as a question."[6] He further develops this mystical sense when he quotes the late Justice Leonard Hand: "The mark of a free person is that ever growing inner uncertainty as to whether or not you are right."[7] This essential attitude of curiosity is one of a cluster of characteristics that, when appropriately developed, constitute a radical commitment to change. The cluster includes anger, imagination, sense of humor, discipline, singleness of purpose, native intelligence, an organized personality, as well as curiosity. It is by integrating these characteristics that the organizer will be best able to promote the approach articulated and implemented in the preorganizing phase of the process.

Believing in people, the radical organizes them so that they will have the power and opportunity to meet each unforeseeable crisis as they move ahead in their eternal search for equality, justice, freedom, peace, a deeper concern for the preciousness of human life, and all the rights and values propounded by our religious traditions.

For Alinsky, "all revolutionary movements are primarily generated from spiritual values and consideration of justice, equality, and peace."[8] Once again affirming his creation-centered approach, he speaks out against the dualism embedded in our culture: "The prime illusion we must rid ourselves of is the conventional view in which things are seen as separate from their counterparts. . . . Everything must be seen as the inevitable partner of its converse, light and darkness, good and evil, life and death . . . and so with every component of the universe; all are paired in this enormous Noah's Ark of life."[9] It is, therefore, out of a collapsing of this dualism that harmony, which results from the building of the organization, is brought forth and finds its expression in power, the ability to act from within and among: "Power is the very essence, the dynamo of life . . . providing a unified strength for a common purpose."[10]

Alinsky restates the creation-centered dimension of his approach and the focus of the introductory or preorganizing phase this way: "It is this awakening of our people from the abysmal apathy" that will awaken us to a "sense of ourselves, as members of the human family,"[11] so that we can move from "the dull gray monotonous road of existence . . . into a brilliantly lit avenue of hope . . . the future of humankind."

The sense of value and dignity that can come to people when they are acknowledged and recognized is recorded in the following excerpt from my journal during a community-organizing experience. It is also true that this approach can be the starting point for personal, social, and ecological justice (geo-justice).

> Another such experience was a meeting between the public works commissioner of the city and a delegation of the Public Works Committee of the Riverdale Community Organization in Toronto's East End. I was a staff person with the delegation. The commissioner, who had previously said he would not attend a public meeting, agreed to go to the East End to discuss the issues with the people of Riverdale. That night I learned that an official's mind can be changed, that people do have power, and that an organizer can obtain satisfaction out of a victory. Change takes place when people become aware of their dignity, value, and ability to act.[12]

The Disorganizing Phase

The second phase of the organizing process is the disorganizing phase. The goal here is to shake things up in the community. This is accomplished when patterns of power that exist at the service of the status quo are scrambled and disorganized in order to prepare for a new kind of structure that can be put to the service of people and Earth. This phase is described in Alinsky's *Reveille for Radicals:*

> The building of People's Organizations with attitudes and purposes that differ from the prior conceptions and attitudes of the local agencies . . . must undergo a period of disorganization in order to make way for the new values, and new purposes. This period of transition is a period of disorganization.[13]

The approach to this phase is summarized in the following axiom. The first step in community organization is community disorganization.

For Alinsky, "organization is in the last analysis disorganization."[14] He is pointing out that the development of a people's organization inevitably involves letting go of attitudes, philosophies, and programs in order to set the stage for "new alignments, new definitions of values and objectives."[15]

In exploring the disorganizing phase of developing an organization, Alinsky uses the analogy of water. Just as hydrogen and oxygen need to let go of their identities in order to form water, so it is necessary that the diverse elements of the community be brought together so that they may comprise an appropriate constellation for the new community organization.

The birth of this new organization, the revolution, is preceded by a letting go of attitudes of heart and mind, a reformation. "It is most important for those of us who want revolutionary change to understand that revolution must be preceded by reformation . . . a radical change in the principles, opinions, sentiments, and affections of the people."[16]

The disorganizing phase of community organization involves a letting go of the need for instant results. "The building of the parts is a tough, tedious, time-consuming, often monotonous and frequently frustrating job."[17]

The disorganizing phase also involves a willingness to step aside and allow people to take the power. This is exemplified in a comment Alinsky made to a group of seminarians in Chicago some forty years ago, "When you go out that door, just make your own personal decision about whether you want to be a bishop or a priest, and everything else will follow."[18]

Alinsky addressed the same question when he said, "The organizer recedes from the local circle of decision makers. This response to questions about what they think becomes a nondirecting counter question, 'What do you think?' His work becomes one of weaning the group from any dependency upon him. Then his work is done."[19] Alinsky also explains that in the early development of the organization, the organizer needs to let go of any subjective involvement and support the people in their developing maturity. As organizers, we also must be willing to let go of the resignation and fatalism that resides within each of us, and get in touch with the hope that burns deep within. "Thermopolitically they are a mass of cold ashes of resignation and fatalism; but inside there are glowing embers of hope which can be fanned by the building of means of obtaining power. Once the power begins, the flame will follow."[20]

In building a community organization, we must be ready to let go of structure and predictability: "There are no fixed chronological points or definite issues. The demands are always changing; the situation is fluid and ever shifting." Many of the goals "are psychological and constantly changing."[21]

Part of the psychological shift is that organizers be able to let go of the people who have been helped and not react to their inevitable resentment. "The organizer knows that it is a human characteristic that someone who asks for help and gets it reacts not only with gratitude but with subconscious hostility toward the one who provided the help."[22]

The continuing need for openness and flexibility on the part of organizers shows up when organizers let go of a rigid role and see themselves as students as well as teachers. Organizers must be willing to change and be changed by the organizing process.

In an interview a short time before he died, Alinsky reflected on the meaning of letting go and letting be for his life as an organizer:

> Suddenly it came to me . . . as a deep gut revelation, that someday I was going to die . . . Once you accept your own mortality, on the deepest level, your life can take on a whole new meaning. . . . You won't care any more about how much money you've got or what people think of you . . . whether you're successful or unsuccessful, important or insignificant. You just care about living every day to the full, drinking in every new experience and sensation as eagerly as a child, and with the same sense of wonder.[23]

In reflecting on Alinsky's thought, we see that both personally and politically letting go and letting be lead to creativity and new life. This point of view is summarized in one of the axiomatic statements of Alinsky's: "If you push a negative hard enough and deep enough, it will break through into its counter side."[24] This view, which is deep in Alinsky's thought, is clearly enunciated in the concluding sentence of *Rules for Radicals*, a statement intended as a doorway to freedom and creativity for us all: "We must believe that it is the darkness before the dawn of a beautiful new world; we will see it when we believe it."[25]

A journal entry from the time of my work as a staff organizer with the Riverdale Community Organization marks the beginning of an action that illustrates the potential for creativity that is available when we are willing to let go personally and structurally of whatever holds us back and look creatively toward the future.

> LCW (Larchmont, Caroline and Winfield) was formed on September 23, at a meeting attended by upward of forty people. The first of many issues decided upon for discussions was that of absentee landlords, specifically the case of the owners of the two homes on Caroline Avenue.[26]

When neither of these landlords showed up at the next meeting, September 30, a dozen of us traveled to the distant upper-class neighborhood home of one of them. It was a cold night, and we huddled together outside while two went in to prepare the way. The rest soon followed, and the living room became the arena.

The owner's excuses, such as, "My husband is in the hospital," were countered by focusing on the bad conditions at the houses on Caroline

Avenue. One member of the delegation said, "There have been three fires here. You could be responsible for burning down our whole neighborhood."

To the owner's comment, "How can you keep up houses in that area?", the group responded, "What do you mean 'that area'?" The landlady pointed to one person in the group, "You look like the smart one!" The people came back, "Are you saying that the rest of us are stupid?" The outcome was a verbal commitment from the owner to do some repairs. On the way home, the group members were so excited by the taste of victory that they wanted to go after the second landlord, even though it was already 10:30 P.M. (they decided against it).

A letter was sent to the landlady to seal the commitment she had made. Within a few days, the garages were repaired, and soon thereafter the interiors of the houses were improved.

The Organizing Phase

The organizing phase refers to creating new organizational units around issues that previously have not been responded to in the structures of the community. It is in this organizing phase that the community itself develops its capacity to act on behalf of transformation.

In his introduction to *Reveille for Radicals,* Alinsky applies the concept of creativity to the ongoing process: "An organizer for a Free and Open Society must be a creative person; his search for universals means the fulfillment of the highest goals of a creative mind—the finding of similarities in seemingly different or similar things in our world."[27] Continuing on this theme of creativity and its application to the organizing process, he writes: "The organizer is driven by the desire to create. The organizer is in a true sense searching for the highest level for which a man can reach—to create, to be a great creator."[28] In another place Alinsky states, "The organizer is a highly imaginative and creative architect and engineer."[29]

In examining Alinsky's thought about creativity, we see an amazing convergence with Meister Eckhart as he acknowledges the deep need that each person has to express his or her creativity, "the passionate desire of all human beings to feel that they have personally contributed to the creation and securing of any objective they desire."[30]

Once again, he enunciates the need for a creative component in the organization phase of building a People's Organization: "The building of a People's Organization is the creation of a new set of realignments, new definitions of values and objectives, the breaking down of prejudices and barriers of all the many other changes that flow out of a people's organization."[31] Creativity involves the personal and social conditions that foster and promote the process. "It is in these contradictions and their incessant interacting tensions that creativity begins," he writes.

In probing more deeply the notion of creativity/breakthrough, Alinsky describes the organization as the vehicle of birth and participation in it as the birth certificate for a new life. "The organization is born out of the issues, and the issues are born out of the organization. . . . Through the organization and its power he will get his birth certificate for life. . . . Things will change from the darkness of a life where all that changes is the calendar."[32]

Bringing a new organization into existence is a concrete example of the creative process. While involved in an ongoing community project in northern Toronto, I wrote in my journal:

> The rapid growth of the northern part of the Borough of Etobicoke (the rate is twice as fast as the remainder of the Borough) has hindered the development of effective lines of communication. Very few community action groups exist in this area, which also contains 80 percent of the Borough's share of Ontario Housing units (public housing). Residents struggle with the problems of high-density living and the lack of supporting social and recreational services. There is a feeling among residents that this part of the Borough is neglected by municipal government.[33]

These feelings were brought to a meeting organized by a resident of the area who was frustrated in her attempt to reduce the size of a nursing home. At this meeting, local groups and individuals expressed their concerns and explored the possibility of the formation of a joint action group to deal with the problems of the Northern Etobicoke area. Twelve people volunteered to work toward establishing an action council. The group met regularly and took action on the nursing home issue. CANE's (Community Action in Northern Etobicoke) case has been brought to the provincial level of government. CANE also took action to help fight pollution problems with residents of the Berry Creek area, and support was also given to the Finch Avenue extension group.

While action was being taken, the group met to work out problems encountered in trying to pull together groups and individuals. The group worked to foster a spirit of cooperation and mutual support. They began to recognize the realities of the task they had undertaken and the special problems of the area, among them the segmentation of residential areas. It became clear that strong organizational support was needed.

The group reflected on recent events and explored new ideas. It also sought leadership and support in order to bring people together around common concerns and action, to influence decisions that affected their lives.

The Reorganizing Phase

In this phase, the new units that recently have been created are brought into structural connection with the previously existing organizational units. The intention of bringing together this new mass-based organization is to exercise sufficient unified power on behalf of the agreed-upon agenda of the people.

The meaning of the interconnectedness and interdependence of compassion finds its expression for Alinsky in the sense of the identification with the pain of all people. "The radical is deeply committed to justice, which finds expression in moral outrage when people's rights are violated. It is this vision and the outrage that give birth to a just and compassionate existence. We seek a world in which the worth of the individual is recognized . . . the creation of the kind of society where all potentialities could be realized; a world where people could live in dignity, security, happiness, and peace—a world based on a morality of humankind."[34]

In continuing to paint his vision of a transformed society, Alinsky writes: "The radical is dedicated to the destruction of the roots of all fears, frustrations, and insecurity of all people, whether they be material or spiritual. . . . The radical places human rights above property rights—when judged on the basis of ideals, philosophy, and objectives . . . a living definition of consistency."[35]

The idea of compassionate interdependence and justice is made concrete when he writes, "If a People's Organization were to be thought of as a tree, the indigenous leaders would be the roots, and the people themselves, the soil."[36]

Alinsky is committed to justice for the *anawim:* "The issue to be resolved is the creation of a world for the little people, a world where the millions instead of the few can live in dignity, peace, and security."[37] Alinsky has passed the torch for a just society to a future generation.

Such transformation can occur. The following quotation appeared in a neighborhood newspaper in Chicago's Garfield Ridge. The article is a report of the community convention of the Midway Organization.

> In an American revolution on the southwest side, the Boss replaces the King as the object of defiance, and the throne room moves to the fifth floor of City Hall, but the reason for dissent remains the same—repugnant taxation.[38]

The residents wanted a return of their tax dollars in the form of service— schools, parks, health facilities, libraries, and other city services. They believed that the current lack of such services was both inadequate and unjust. I served as a staff person in this process, and I am convinced that the organizing process produced transformation. This organizing effort gave birth to the Midway Organization in Southwest Chicago, established to carry out and coordinate the policies and issues of the Midway community. From this new base, the people were free to determine a resolution to the problems and issues that confronted them. Because of their new voice, a factory (Corbett Steel) agreed to reduce the noise pollution. Another (Union Carbide) agreed to decrease the amount of resins that were being released into the air. Another positive result occurred when a railway company agreed to fill an empty ditch and build a fence along the railway to provide a safer place for children.

The responsibility and privilege of every organizer is to "design and execute a new structure in a new community,"[39] a community that is born out of conflict and gives birth to a free and open society in which the major theme is a "harmony of dissonance."

"The function of an organizer," according to the Industrial Areas Foundation (IAF) Saul Alinsky Training Institute states, "is to raise questions that agitate, that break through the accepted patterns."[40] It is this breakthrough that gives birth to the vision Alinsky announced more than forty years ago: "Let the cry sound again, clearly, boldly, shattering the deathlike silence of decay.... Let its echoes go beyond and shake the hearts of oppressors everywhere.... A vision will come to the eyes of the millions who dwell in dingy New York tenements ... and to all people."[41]

Community organization builds a constellation of relationships that have the capacity for action from an ever-increasing base. The resultant organization can be visualized as a three-dimensional cluster of relationships. These new organizations become mediating structures that can handle the flow of information and make change more possible.

Organization doesn't just happen. Some principles of organization include the following.

- Focus on relationship; the organization mirrors our worldview.
- Be aware of everyone involved in the constellation of relationships. True revolution begins in the heart as well as in the structure.
- Involve as many people as possible in the actions.
- Build the base as a foundation for action.
- Negotiate with the person or people who have the power to resolve the problem.
- Involve participants in actions; experiencing the resistance of those in power radicalizes and converts.
- Strive for a dialectical consciousness, embracing the paradox and synthesis in apparent contradictions.

Community organization is a mass educational project that is an expression of direct action through collective leadership. Through synthesis and study, people are able to act at the deepest level of their values and visions in order to create and shape the future. The organizer is an artist who, through listening and recognition, pieces together a quilt of relationships that enhances harmony, balance, and peace.

FOR REFLECTION

All revolutionary movements are primarily generated from spiritual values and consideration of justice, equality, and peace.

The prime illusion we must rid ourselves of is the conventional view in which things are seen as separate from their counterparts. . . . Everything must be seen as the inevitable partner of its converse, light and darkness, good and evil, life and death . . . and so with every component of the universe; all are paired in this enormous Noah's Ark of life.[42]

It is this awakening of our people from the abysmal apathys[43] [that will awaken us to a] sense of ourselves, as members of the human family, [so that we can move from] the dull gray monotonous road of existence . . . into a brilliantly lit avenue of hope . . . the future of humankind.

It is most important for those of us who want revolutionary change to understand that revolution must be preceded by reformation . . . a radical change in the principles, opinions, sentiments, and affections of the people.[44]

The issue to be resolved is the creation of a world for the little people, a world where the millions instead of the few can live in dignity, peace, and security.

The function of an organizer [the IAF Saul Alinsky Training Institute states] is to raise questions that agitate, that break through the accepted patterns. [It is this breakthrough that gives birth to the vision Alinsky announced more than forty years ago] Let the cry sound again, clearly, boldly, shattering the deathlike silence of decay. . . . Let its echoes go beyond and shake the hearts of oppressors everywhere. . . . A vision will come to the eyes of the millions who dwell in dingy New York tenements . . . and to all people.

—Saul Alinsky

We need to develop new approaches . . . not management but encouragement, not control but genesis—information is the solar energy of organization.

—Margaret Wheatley[45]

Education: The Art of Transformation

Human consciousness comes into the world as a flaming ball of imagination. . . . The secret of good teachers is to regard the child's intelligence as a fertile field in which seeds may be sown to grow under the flaming heat of his imagination.

—Maria Montessori

Education is a context in which to discover our place in the universe. It is praxis—action and reflection upon our world, whereby we become aware of the constraint in our lives and take action to transform the situation. Education is about knowledge that is organic, liberating, and free; it is a process of discovery, self-discovery, and action. The primary textbook for our new knowing is our own experience and the book of Earth. Sharing what we have learned becomes a touchstone of authentic education. At its deepest level, education is an eruption into awareness and action from the wellsprings of our souls. At its root, education is about evocation and celebration: it activates the genetic memory of our connection to an evolving universe, its origins, mystery, and unfolding. We understand this cellular relationship through science, experience it in our spiritual practice, and express it in our creativity, particularly the creation of compassion.

Earth is our textbook, our teacher, and our classroom. This perspective brings together now-isolated disciplines (law, religion, psychology, economics, education, art, science) that oppose one another and the planet upon which we live. When we see Earth as primary and other wisdoms as derivative, we can begin to reinvent the meaning of *learning* and discover a new kind of integration. Education becomes a way of making the human sensitive to the communication and the revelations of Earth. No longer negative inculturation and conformity to an unjust system, it is the process of recognizing our role in the unfolding universe at this present moment. Education can free us from imposed patterns and presuppositions; it can be an adventure filled with fascination that invites us into creative and compassionate action.

In our liberation, we realize that through our communication with the natural world we are functioning within the larger context of Earth community. Stunned by the wonder of seeing Earth as a whole from the window of a spaceship and peering into the vast emptiness of subatomic particles, we are thrilled to know that the world is alive, and so are we.

Deep learning is about the way we live, and think, and act, and are together. It is an adventure that requires courage and risk taking, because in the process something dies and something is born. Deep learning's focus is not management by objectives; it is liberation and change of heart. Both teachers and students are called to demonstrate and experience respect, reverence, and responsibility. The results of deep learning are both disruptive and creative.

One way to approach deep learning is *conscientization*, Paulo Freire's contribution to liberation. I had the opportunity to study with Freire and to collaborate with his colleagues from the Institute for Cultural Action, at that time based within the World Council of Churches in Geneva. I felt then, as I do now, that Freire's work in education has been a monumental contribution to our culture, a process designed for freedom and critical awareness. As Freire expresses it, conscientization refers to the critical reflection on reality in order to transform it. Creative action happens when we perceive reality as subject to transformation. In the process, we name our experience and become subjects of our own existence; we take possession of our reality, demythologize it, and act on it for the sake of liberation. Conscientization culminates in cultural action; there are several components to this process.

Descriptive Phase

The participants are invited to say who they are and tell their stories. Their dignity and value is recognized and acknowledged. They become subjects of their own destiny. Their stories organize their experience in a shareable way as they name the problems, concerns, questions, and contradictions in their lives.

The awareness that results from the narrating of their experience assists the participants to acquire an incredible sense of self-esteem. One of the participants illustrates this when he says, "Tomorrow I will do my work with pride; I know that I am worthwhile."[46]

Some themes that have been generated through my own work with this process are: stereotypes between men and women; barriers around race, religion, gender, class, and sexual identity; and relationship to cultural pathology, ecological devastation, and consciousness.

Interpretive Phase

As they tell their stories, the participants come to understand their oppression, the internal and structural obstacles that hold them back. A visual and verbal depiction of this oppression is called a code. When they reflect on these codes and ask questions about them, they begin to interpret their oppression. These questions may be what do they see, feel, have done, need to do, or need to know. The capacity to interpret our own pathologies requires that we let go of the consciousness of oppression in order to be alive to move toward action for freedom. Freire describes it this way: "The teachers must die as teachers, little by little, they cannot decree their own death; they can only be killed by the students little by little in the process."[47]

As an example, participants in this process have named two aspects of their experience of oppression: the pressure to conform to external expectations rather than to follow their deepest convictions; and the temptation to be caught up in the consumerism of society rather than respond to the authentic needs of self, other, and Earth.

Cultural Action Phase

Cultural action involves responding to the concerns and problems through actions that can both heal and transform. Creating action, it teaches us and brings about change.

Freire states it this way: "We cannot create knowledge without acting. The focus of the action is to transform the world"; and "Education is an act of creation capable of unlearning other creative acts, a process from the inside out."[48]

Participants in my workshops have named it this way: "The realization of the need to articulate and express the creative process through action," and "the need to overcome fear and engage in creative action to transform our lives, culture, and ecology."

Conscientization — Critical Reflection for Transformation

Education is not simply knowing but invoking transformation that is the result of the action. Freire describes the process this way: "Education for liberation, as a true praxis, is an act of knowing and a method of transforming action which people have to exercise on the reality which they seek to know."[49]

To achieve this authentic consciousness, conscientization confronts traditional education, which separates teaching from practice, teacher from student, and people from the world. Alternatively, it proposes a synthesis in which teachers become students, students become teachers, and the classroom becomes the street and the natural world. From Freire's perspective, education is an invitation to read and write our own cosmic story. It is a doorway that channels our creative energy into a new global community. It becomes a basis for cultural action, a breakthrough into a new awareness that empowers us to give birth to the universe and ourselves. Conscientization is a healing of dualisms: the separation of theory from practice; the separation of existing knowledge from the creating of new knowledge; and the separation of teaching from learning, of educating from being educated.

The authentic praxis that results from this deep learning is understood as cultural action for freedom. We place ourselves outside the huge cultural computer that programs our lives and achieve an increased capacity to listen, see, perceive, and act. We discover a coherence between theory and practice, between what we say and what we do. Knowledge becomes a process and not a package; it is created and recreated, never transferred. We avoid becoming cynical or bureaucratic, striving instead for truth with acceptance of both our strengths and our limitations. As the hand adjusts to the stone in order to throw it, so we adjust to the culture in order to transform it.

Conscientization asserts that it is not possible to separate consciousness from the object of consciousness; thus, there is constant interaction between thinking persons, the culture, and Earth that envelops them. "To utter our word" is to name reality as a combination of thought and action; the awareness of reality and self-awareness become one event.

Paulo Freire's *Conscientization: Education for Cultural Action* has enormous implications for society and spirituality. Conscientization names for each of us the experience of learning and is congruent with the human journey. Freire's approach to learning is congruent with our spiritual journey and the basis of transformative action for our culture.

FOR REFLECTION

The educational process can be experiential, participatory, and transforming; to foster active involvement through seeing, judging, acting, reviewing and celebrating . . . to respond to the challenges of human development, solidarity and building the civilization of love.

—Santa Domingo and Beyond[50]

Education is not for life, education is life.

—Rabbi Heschel

We cannot create knowledge without acting; the focus of the action is to transform the world, to establish interdependent relationships with human beings, with the cosmos and with God.[51]

Conscientization is an act of creation capable of unleashing other creative acts, a process from the inside out, an action of the learner himself, with the educator collaborating and nothing more.[52]

Every relationship of domination, of exploitation, is by definition violent whether or not the violence is addressed by drastic means. In such a relationship, dominator and dominated alike are reduced to things . . . the former dehumanized by an excess of power, the latter by a lack of it.[53]

—Paulo Freire

Psychology: Healing the Heart, Celebrating the Soul

Ordinary human life is not ordinary at all, but in fact, highly dramatic, a field of conflict between forces of self-destruction and power—unexpected powers of creativity and new life.

—Gregory Baum[54]

I first began to examine the marvels of the interior life when I entered therapy in Toronto. After attending a conference for Young Christian Students and Young Christian Workers, I drove into Toronto's downtown area for my first session. As the weeks went by, I felt buoyant and encouraged. I began to find language and expression for the unnamed "upset" that was in some way rumbling around inside me. Along with many others with backgrounds in theology and religion, I was searching to find expression in community and relationship for the aspirations that were boiling up from the increased expectations that had surfaced in a post-Vatican II church.

As I reflect back upon that experience, I realize that after the initial phase of giving voice to my problems, the more extended goals of insight, working through, and resolution remained uncertain. I see now that the psychoanalytic approach I encountered viewed the psyche as matter. In a sense, the psyche was a suitcase filled with repressed feelings, and the goal of therapy was to unpack the suitcase. Although I moved forward, there was no completion of the process. It was like bailing out a leaky boat—the leak didn't stop. I can see now that the long-term process engaged in by many of us was, and remains, a reflection of the limitations of a Freudian-based approach, buried within the confines of a mechanistic worldview. Still, much was accomplished.

I am convinced that for many in Canada and the United States, therapy is important, perhaps necessary, as we strive to deal with the intense alienation and fragmentation of everyday life. Our experience of therapy following Vatican II generated much hope in my own life and in the lives of many who remain my dearest friends. These friendships were fashioned, and our creativity supported, in ways unimaginable without such an opportunity.

One day after a group therapy session, a student made the following comment to the teacher: "Lea, how did you become such a creative therapist?" Lea's answer has remained with me as a statement of spiritual depth: "In my life I have known deep joy and profound pain; those are my primary credentials."

Although grateful for the hope and friendships of that first encounter with therapy, I am still searching for an understanding of the psyche and a therapeutic process that is more attuned to my deeper intuitions. Many today are on this search. Our approach to the spiritual journey includes a therapeutic quest but reaches a point where a different worldview is necessary. The two experiences and approaches can work together in the context of the universe story.

An Expanded Worldview

The universe came into being fifteen billion years ago and continues to unfold, marking the evolution of awareness, mind, and consciousness. The universe has released energy that has a capacity for consciousness, recounted in the universe's story and remembered in the word of rock, tree, and mammal. The capacity for awareness, to know that we know, is the greatest gift of humankind. It is also a source of much destruction and devastation.

Recent insights in physics and the legacy of mystics of all traditions (strange bedfellows in an earlier view) have much to teach us about consciousness as a source of action and transformation. We have begun to see the psyche as an abode of the spiritual, a place of profound healing, a source of creativity, a context for mysticism, and the locus of interconnectedness and relationships. The quest for oneness enables us to savor beauty and quench our thirst for meaning, purpose, and interconnectedness.

Research and reflection on the meaning of consciousness reveal that the mind is not a container of repressed forces but a cosmological context that shares its boundaries with the universe itself, a constellation of attractions and memories that mirror and celebrate the deepest aspirations of the human journey. Our capacity to know that we know puts us in touch with our cosmic origins, the beauty of Earth, the pain of the cosmos, and the surprise of the wonderful relatedness to all of life. This capacity for awareness rescues the psyche from being perceived as an object to be probed and returns it to a context for adventure and celebration of human and planetary potential. Our understanding of the capacity to know has transformed our efforts for change. No longer are the psyche, society, or the universe perceived as building blocks of matter to be moved or destroyed. Rather, we look at all three as processes of transformation, and we celebrate their continuous unfolding. From this perspective, the psyche, Earth, and the cosmos become the components of an ongoing Divine story leading to justice for the planet and deep cultural therapy for its people.

In the unconscious wells of the psyche, our connection to the sacredness of all of life deepens; we contact both fear and beauty. We acknowledge the experiences that come to us from feelings, spirituality, and Earth. We experience an awakening to memories and moments that transcend space and time. In our interaction with the natural world, we find the nourishment our psyches need and an ever-deepening appreciation for the subtleties of emptiness and magnitude. We celebrate an awareness of our uniqueness within the unity of all that is. We find the continuing invitation to go deeper, to exercise our self-reflection. We acknowledge and activate the properties of self-healing that result from the ripples of awareness that resonate from deep within the cosmos.

Our awakening to this knowing calls us to act and be constantly reborn. This ever-emerging awareness enfolds the energy of the universe into patterns of genesis and transformation. The psyche of the cosmos becomes a reflection of the divine mind and a pattern for the culture we feel called to create. From this perspective, awareness is not so much interacting with a reservoir of repression as it is a galaxy of archetypal images that invite us to a cosmic dance. Our investigation of the psyche spans a wide spectrum of interest and engagement.

Theodore Roszak writes in *The Voice of Earth*, "A culture that can do so much to damage the planetary fabric that sustains it and yet continues along its unimpeded course is mad with the madness of a deadly compulsion that reaches beyond our own kind, to all the brute innocence about us."[55] As we celebrate with him the knowledge that our bodies contain "salt from the ocean and ash from the stars," we begin to realize more fully that our psyches and our souls have literally been cradled in the hands of the Divine. This newly acquired wisdom points to the need to heal the alienation between people and Earth. We must become responsible for Earth—healed of our aggression toward the planet and its people. Coming to understand our cosmic and biological origins on the levels of cosmos, dream, conception, and birth (the perinatal process of the soul) helps us become instruments of personal and planetary peace. The world around us is external to our body but not outside our mind. We are, in fact, connected to all. This sea of wonder is the psyche, the context of wholeness and health. At this level of understanding, we can say with Dom Helder Camara that there is a realization of the Divine in all things and no basis for anything but peace.

I have come to see that an expanded view of psychology can assist us in removing the barriers to mysticism, giving us a deeper comprehension of our true nature, an experience of belonging to something greater than ourselves, and an increased sense of our place in the universe. This shift away from determinism makes it possible for us to transcend traditional human boundaries and see the universe as the context of our journey.

Eco-psychology

Each of us has been touched by the beauty of birds, meadows, beaches, blossom; they have reminded us of the Divine and revealed much about ourselves. Whether it be the beaches of Ireland, the coastline of Australia, the starkness of the Andes, or the barges sailing the Potomac, the sights smells, and sounds of our lives have taught us much about who we are and what we do.

The emerging wisdom of eco-psychology teaches us about who we are in relationship to the natural world. We begin to notice, for example, how our experience of a canyon says much about our connection to shelter and being protected. Each experience of the natural world touches us in a special way. In other words, our connections to Earth have lessons for us.

As eco-psychologist Allen Kanner points out, "The area of psychology (eco-psychology) focuses on the emotional bond between humans and the rest of the natural world."[56] This approach strives to heal the separation between humans and the natural world, which accelerated during the Industrial Age. It rescues people from the impulse to control and dominate other humans and the natural world.

Today, eco-psychologists are guiding people through experiences of the "wilderness" (the natural world); these "eco-plunges," extended periods of living gently on the land, activate participants' insights and energy about how people change and how they can contribute to life on our planet in a more peaceful way. Others teach and guide groups in restoration work; in this process they form deep bonds with each other and Earth. The traditional "office" or "chair" therapy is becoming a context where clients are encouraged to go on a hike, participate in walking meditation to "slow down and smell the roses" as they extend their awareness and relationship to the natural world.

All of these forms are confronting the value-laden and culturally determined aspects of the psyche. We begin to notice, for example, that toxic dump sites are located in neighborhoods that house minority people. We become increasingly aware of the connection between advertising, which falsely inflates our desire for the endless acquisition of products, and our chronic lack of self-esteem. Not only are our authentic human needs denigrated by this approach, but the result is a flood of consumerism and waste that both pollutes the planet and cripples the psyche. Eco-psychology is a great gift in this time of transition, an important dimension of the language of the universe, whereby we can heal the planet and ourselves.

The Challenge of Soul-Making

What have I learned from therapy? I have learned that it is possible to connect with and understand the forces that would otherwise determine my choices without my awareness. The experience of being marginalized through my childhood has made it possible to value living on the edge, for I believe that is a place of creativity. This has been my experience in relationship to church, school, and other facets of my life. I was forced to develop parallel structures, and this has become a life strategy that I have become aware of during therapy.

I have learned—and come to accept—that the experience of upset does not necessarily point toward pathology. Often it can be an impulse toward balance, harmony, and psychic justice. A dancer told me once that the creative process in her work was moving from being off the center toward the center. The same is true in the emotional life. There is turbulence caused in the psyche, in fact in the whole person, during a movement from imbalance to balance. Problems and pain are also sources of wholeness and healing.

I have learned that therapy can end. The need to be healed and then healed some more comes from our conviction that we are fatally flawed and will never be healed. A new perspective on psychology and a spirituality of blessing has taught me that healing is possible and that therapy need not be endless.

Psychology also has taught me that in our individual lives we recognize that we are both private selves and public persons and that there is no hard boundary between one and the other. I see that the integral relationship between the individual and the group is of tremendous importance.

Psychology teaches us about healing and self-discovery; about meaning, purpose, and destiny; about how patterns of the past and indicators for the future converge and amplify our capacity to embrace and express the present moment. Within the deep recesses of the soul is the cradle of creativity. We learn to appreciate difference so that what emerges from within is not a mere duplication of what has gone before; here, we confront the depth of our mortality and experience resurrection in our souls, a resurrection that finds expression in the beauty of celebration.

FOR REFLECTION

When religion lost the cosmos, humankind became neurotic and invented psychology.

—Otto Rank[57]

The best and most beautiful things in the world cannot be seen or even touched, they must be felt in the heart.

—Helen Keller

We teach children how to measure, how to weigh. We fail to teach them how to revere, how to sense wonder and awe. The sense of the sublime, the sign of inward greatness of the human soul and something which is potentially given to all men is a rare gift.

—Rabbi Abraham Heschel

Deep Ecology: To Wake Up One Day Different

Deep ecology concerns those personal moods, values, aesthetic and philosophical convictions which serve no necessarily utilitarian, nor rational end. By definition their sole justification rests upon the goodness, balance, truth and beauty of the natural world, and of a human being's biological and psychological need to be fully integrated with it.

—Michael Tobias[58]

The image of standing at the precipice of the new millennium, of bailing out a leaky boat, and of turning around and beginning again are about focus, reflection, and results.

Virginia Griffin in *Eros of Everyday Life* reminds us that canaries were once taken down into the mines to see if the air was toxic. Today, many people who are sensitive to the toxicity of our historical moment are becoming "canaries of the culture."

Whatever our individual approach, each action will be designed to promote a lifestyle and a culture that is aligned to the wisdom of Earth and the rhythms of the biosphere. Each of us will be motivated by a deep love for the planet and filled with gratitude for the vast array of beauty reflected in the fall leaves, the delicious berries and fruits that come forth in the seasons, and the rich diversity that flows forth through the presence of the simple beauty of a fawn, a stately maple, fertile black soil, and fresh flowing water.

This approach to focused action is often referred to as "deep ecology." As anthropologist Lisa Faithorn describes it, deep ecology

recognizes our planet Earth as a natural living system, as a biosphere in which all things are interconnected. It is the spiritual, intellectual, emotional, physical exploration and practice of biocentrically based, ecologically sustainable, socially just relationships among all humans and between humans and other forms of nature.[59]

The practice of deep ecology is a "homecoming"—coming home to a self that can be understood as coextensive with the biosphere, an identity whereby our being is sensitized and attuned to the living systems of Earth. The pain of the trees when attacked by the saw for clear-cutting touches us, for example, and we are moved to respond. Deep ecology also brings us home to ourselves, our ancestors, and our lineage. We borrow from the wisdom of other traditions and learn to research and celebrate our ancestors and create sacredness through attentiveness to meditation and mindfulness.

My own life has been enriched by my sister's research into our family's Irish and French roots. Having visited Ireland and the former farms and grave sites of my ancestors in Canada, I feel a deeper sense of connection to the land and my people.

Homecoming is profoundly affected by our connection to the places on the planet where we grew up and live now—our bioregions. The rivers, trees, and landscape are indelible poetry for our souls. I remember with gratitude and depth my connection to the bioregion of my birth and feel nourished today by memories of gardens, rivers, and land.

Deep ecology challenges us to find our bearings in relationship to Earth itself, to celebrate creation as the center of existence, and to express gratitude for the interconnectedness of all things. In our awareness of deep ecology, we also acknowledge the rights of other life forms to flourish while sustaining their integrity and purpose.

We look to the future through the eyes of rainforest activist John Seed, who says that we need to awaken tomorrow entirely different. Our actions must be guided by the wisdom that emerges from our ecological self and fostered by a community of kindred spirits. They will respond to the question, "Who are we and what we are called to do right now?" These actions will touch the heart of the universe and evoke a genetic memory of beauty and balance to move us forward into a deeper experience of mystery and meaning.

Economics: If the economy is up, how can the Earth community be down?

> Green economics calls traditional "growth is good" assumptions into question.
> —Paul Ekins[60]

We are called to renew the face of Earth. To carry out this task and live with integrity into a sustainable future, we must know our ancestors and make decisions with future generations in mind. Yet, today these deeper values have been displaced by an ethic whose primary thrust is to augment money, production, and consumption; constant increase has become the law of an economics that drives our culture. King Midas has become the architect of greed that drives this moment, while "jobless growth" has become a mantra for our time. The gap between the haves and the have-nots grows increasingly. We must develope a new relationship with the economy and with creation.

When we begin to hear the "cry of creation," we become aware of toxic water and poisoned fish as small examples of the total planetary plundering and destruction. Our hope is to become free from poisoning and stench. Indeed, our hope becomes a lamentation for the damage we have done, engagement in the nonviolent struggle, conversion and a belief in the capacity to change. Hope can help us discover new ways to develop health care, education, taxation, public transportation, and housing. Hope becomes a vehicle for liberation, a creative energy that invites participation and empowers us. Hope becomes the energy of a deep and absolute certitude that evokes a profound embrace of peace, creation, and geo-justice.

This emergence of hope will be fostered when we find new ways to create economic measures that reflect the values that we hold dear. This process will flow from a conviction that "nations' economy and political culture are increasingly at odds with their best values and aspirations and that new thinking is needed to bring them back together" (Redefining Progress, a public policy group based in San Francisco which challenges conventional economics and proposes viable alternatives).

This prophetic statement brings into question the popular notion that growth is an unquestionable good and that more is better. When we view the world through new eyes, we begin to see that our economy is organized in such a way that despite the "good news" reports of the economic indicators, people feel "bad" and experience no enhancement of their quality of life.

Clearly, what is needed, as the project "Redefining Progress" points out, is social and ecological indicators similar to economic ones. Only then will we be able to dispel the illusion that "the rising tide lifts all boats" and begin to look at the real indicators of well-being that affect our lives.

I was involved in a group that gathered to explore this question. We were invited to write on a piece of paper something we believed was overvalued and to draw a symbol of this item. As a bowl was passed around to collect the papers, we talked of our items—money, entertainment, fashion, real estate, and more. Then we were invited to write the name of something we believed was undervalued and place the paper on a dish filled with earth. The responses were moving and prophetic. Participants spoke of women, green space in urban areas, old growth forests, play, natural beauty, health, and more. The responses were encouraging and spoke to the deeper values of people, precisely the values so often ignored in the marketplace of everyday economics. Our final activity that evening was to gather into working groups and prepare a "newscast" to report the movement of genuine program indicators in the culture. The reports spoke of resource depletion, pollution, and long-term environmental damage, along with other deeper values often not measured or reported in the media. I left the room convinced that economics could be moved from a discipline that encourages consumerism and even devastation to one that enhances human existence and supports the integrity of the entire Earth community.

We live in a world where economic rationality creates the illusion of objectivity. Supply and demand and production and consumption have become touchstone categories. The result is a system that overlooks social and ecological benefits and costs. We need to dream of an alternative that honors Earth and every species and become engaged in a process that can bring our dream into reality. Rabbi Michael Lerner, author of *The Politics of Meaning,* holds out the challenge for life and relationships to be built on love and caring rather than consumerism and looking out for Number One as the guides to survival. We must transform our economic sustem that turns children into consumers by the time they are four. We must create a new economics to make it possible for the natural world to recover its health and for humans to participate in the community of life with joy and fulfillment. The words of mythologist Joseph Campbell can guide us:

> Awe is what moves us forward. . . . Society is the enemy when it imposes its structures on the individual. . . . To refuse the call is stagnation. . . . If you follow someone else's way you are not going to realize your potential. . . . The very cage you are afraid to enter is the very thing you are looking for. . . . As you go on the way of life you will see a great chasm. . . . Jump, it is not as wide as you think it is.[61]

A Coalition for Earth

> A coalition for Earth—a call to action and collaboration between those
> who have made an option for the poor with their lives and substance,
> and those who are dedicated to the salvation of the precious resources
> of our small planet Earth.
>
> —Jack Egan[62]

Profound cultural shifts call for imaginative responses. In the medieval
period, women and men living in convents and monasteries discovered
new ways to apply their religious commitment in the face of profound
societal changes. Through the founding and staffing of schools, hospi-
tals, and agencies, they fostered education, health care, and social ser-
vices. As they labored, the infrastructure of a new society was developed.

Many of us remember the Vietnam War, the Civil Rights Movement,
and the urban crises that swept across this country three decades ago. The
resulting movements for peace, racial integration, and urban solidarity
became expressions of a society frozen in fear, overwhelmed by an indus-
trial era, and wounded by race, class, and gender injustice.

These cultural crises gave birth to new programs and approaches.
Urban training centers were begun in the midsixties, followed in 1969
by the Industrial Areas Foundation Saul Alinsky Training Institute. Men
and women learned how to diagnose and respond to problems unprece-
dented to that day. New coalitions and programs began. Jack Egan, then
at the University of Notre Dame, founded the Catholic Committee on
Urban Ministry; this project became a network of women and men,
both inside and outside the nation's churches, committed to social and
economic justice for all. Gino Baroni, later with the Department of
Housing and Urban Development in the Carter Administration, founded
the National Center for Urban Ethnic Affairs in Washington. The Inter-
faith Federation on Community Organization with Lucius Walker was
yet another response.

The Democratic Convention in Chicago in 1968 indicated that the
political agenda of the country had lost its focus; the assassinations of
the Rev. Martin Luther King, Jr., and Robert Kennedy were profound
indicators of a deeply troubled and toxic culture. Increased industrializa-
tion, overcrowding in the cities, competition for jobs, and the inevitable
unemployment contributed to civil unrest and racial turbulence.

Many would say that the mid-nineties are another watershed in
history. The alarm of ecological devastation sounded by Rachel Carson's
Silent Spring in 1962 and repeated a decade later by the Club of Rome
has begun to reach the consciousness of the dominant culture.

The reflections recorded on the first Earth Day in 1970 are now understood by many:

> Poor people have long known what is wrong. . . . A whole society is coming to realize that it must drastically change.[63]

The need for drastic change is becoming manifest in many ways; new initiatives are being undertaken by church groups, nongovernmental organizations, new political parties, environmental programs, academic institutions, corporate alternatives, and others. These programs are bringing hope to many.

It is also true that an agenda of opposition is flourishing across the country. Our hope is that well-developed programs of social and ecological justice will keep hope alive, carrying the next generation forward with confidence in the future. As in the medieval period and in the 60's, our imaginations and moral consciences are being challenged in unprecedented ways.

The publication in 1963 of Harvey Cox's *The Secular City* named the confusion and loss of meaning that resulted from the urban crises. Other books that have captured our moment of challenge are Thomas Berry's *The Dream of Earth* and Leonardo Boff's *Ecology and Liberation*. Today, there is a growing awareness that a new level of cooperation is necessary between those working for social justice in our nation's inner cities and those committed to ecological balance in the natural world. We need both efforts if we are to achieve the common goal of health and wholeness for people and the planet. Now is the time for new actions and new levels of cooperation.

The prophetic challenges of *Silent Spring* and *The Secular City* have converged at this moment of social and ecological crises. From the precipice of millennial fever, a new coalition for social and ecological justice is forming. The new Coalition for Earth, the coming together of people involved in the reinvention of organizing, education, psychology, deep ecology and economics, will guide and support our efforts. Then the wellsprings of our culture will flow with clean water, and the awareness of the sacredness of all things (urban and natural) will penetrate our consciousness and be reflected in our actions. Our generation's challenge is to foster a more intimate connection between humans and the natural world—to discover the sacred dimension in rocks, water, trees, humans, and social institutions. This awakening to sacredness can support and promote new ways to restore the natural world and restructure society.

The actions we must take are varied and profound, but all need to be congruent with Earth. Earth in its beauty and tenderness is alive; our actions must complement the processes that are themselves constantly emerging. Only then will our actions be fostered by a sense of reverence and a sensitivity to the sacred, evoked and energized by the fourfold wisdom of the following:

- the native peoples who live in the universe;
- women's wisdom;
- the classical traditions; and
- the new science.

Energized and encouraged in our actions, we focus on a life of well-being and beauty that emerges from a sense of place. With poet and farmer Wendell Barry, we then can say:

> We will never know who we are
> Until we discover where we are.

As we plan our actions, we discover that deep in our psyches lies a cellular memory of a profound experience of belonging to a particular place on the planet. Our actions will prosper when they cultivate the vital link between the life of the human and a more pervasive vision of life on the planet. As we search in sensitive and nonjudgmental ways for greater understanding, we discover that Earth is the primary reference for all our actions. As Miriam MacGillis says, "Each of us must take our place in the unfolding mystery that is the heart of the universe.[64]

Our convictions are rooted in the capacity to act and make a difference. Corporations *will* listen to us when we withdraw our dollars and literally take our business elsewhere. This is only one way we begin to live the new story and confront the pathological implication of the current cultural story.

True to the story from which it springs, the soulwork of the culture will be an incremental movement from perception to action. Anthropology, psychology, science, art, and economics will need to be revisioned. Through reflection and soulwork, we create that vision and the actions necessary for personal, social, and ecological transformation. We move forward into the future empowered by the collective wisdom necessary to be agents of re-creation and people capable of writing a language for the music of the universe.

Some actions that can move us into the future include:

- changing our lifestyles regarding food, work, housing, and transportation;
- participating in base groups to integrate what we learn, feel, and practice;
- acting from a new vision and propagating the seeds of innovation;
- having new eyes and ears to see and listen to the young of every species;
- being open to the voice that invites us into silence, meditation, and deeper levels of transformation;
- knowing our bioregion, the place where we live, as if for the first time;
- continuing to invite and evoke stories and circles where we celebrate the unpredictable powers that unfold;
- practicing moments of gratitude for beauty, diversity, and connectedness; and
- further developing and implementing organizations such as the Center for the New Millennium, Project Earth, and A Coalition for Earth, as vehicles for geo-justice and cultural rebirth through Earth literacy, dream, story, action, and liberation. [See Appendix C]

How will this new coalition be built? It will emerge from gatherings, stories, and truth. I have spent much of my adult life on the edge of structures, the edge of family, the edge of ideas. People who live on the edge must find their own place of information, support, and possible common action, much as doctors, engineers, and other professionals have their conventions. But where do the people living the new cosmology gather?

Recently a friend asked me that very question. Having studied the new cosmology and a spirituality of Earth, she asked, "What comes next?" My response to her was this: Gather a group of friends who share your vision; tell your dreams and stories; and stay together for the long haul. This is, I believe, what it means to become part of a movement that can carry us into the new millennium. We know that we can do together what we could never do alone. But we need a place of balance, harmony, and peace to help us face a dominant culture that undoubtedly sees us as "far out," "unrealistic," or "out of step."[65]

Living the new cosmology requires a home community to energize and support our vision, to grow a seed of hope in the dark night of our cultural soul, to generate the energy necessary to quench the thirst for an authentic place of influence. Our search for a prophetic community, as Robert Muller, Chancellor of the United Nations University for Peace in Costa Rica, pointed out, "will not be the product of any one person, but will be a collective product . . . the creation of a new human species . . . made up of thousands and thousands of networks."[66]

Our gatherings for action will be fueled by celebration; everything becomes symbol and sacrament. Through celebration we experience a freedom and fulfillment denied us in our lives. Our dreams and stories converge into a common act of liberation.

As we fashion such a movement, I am reminded of the wisdom of Canadian geese. When they fly together, it takes only 70 percent of the energy required to fly alone. They also rotate the position of leader. This is a wonderful example of how shared leadership can promote collective action to build a Coalition for Earth. When we gather with friends, we gain their wisdom and support, and we acquire greater energy and more freedom for the task. We experience a connection between our inner selves and the outer world, and we see both within the context of the natural world. Empowered by our new vision, we are carried forward into a cooperative flight of unity and integration.

In our journey into the new cosmology, we see ourselves claiming our individual identities while being drawn forward into a larger whole; we collapse the dualism between the personal and collective. Looking toward the future, we acknowledge that wisdom is pluralistic; we celebrate the awareness that there are many points of view and different ways of experiencing truth.

As we gather to build a new society, we discover that our approaches and structures must be flexible, experimental, and open to change. In our journey, we relocate the locus of authority and decision-making to the level where people think, feel, and act. We pledge our allegiance to the natural world, realizing that our sacred reality must be in harmony with Earth. How we live the new cosmology will continue to be in dialogue with the findings of science and the deeper questions of Earth literacy as we reflect on the purpose, direction, and meaning in our stories. Theologian Elizabeth Johnson says we are called to be "spiders,"[67] to weave together the interconnected tapestry of life. Sally Helgesen in *The Web of Inclusion* puts it another way: "The process of change is not like an ink stain. . . . It is more like a lot of little splatters that keep getting bigger and bigger and then some of them come together and coalesce."[68] A strategy that assists many of us in our interaction with the culture is to create an institution for ourselves; that is, through telephone, desk, bookshelf, and letterhead, we can develop a profile and perception of our work that is available and understandable to the dominant culture.

As we wake up to the link of the well-being of the human with the quality of life for *all* species, we generate a vision that we hope and trust will energize and support the entire Earth community. Living that vision creates a context for common actions and common consciousness that will foster a new relationship to the natural world, enhance the mystery of existence, and promote a new mode of human functioning.

FOR REFLECTION

A Movement

A Movement
is dance
poetry
music
which follows no metric
yet can be precise in capturing reality.

It awakens our soul
our inner courage
our reason for being.

It calls us to the Cry
Demanding our every passion
tearing down statues built on images of Men
coming to a kaleidoscope of possibilities which finds a new
path in search of the Wild Geese.

It beckons us to be released
defying Norms
making us laugh at ourselves and cry at our fragility.

It asks us to become an Irregular Verb.

It commands us to discipline
Calling us to attention
to be at our stations alert,
tapping our energy and creativity,
while we willingly give
our suffering and defeat
our joy and our laughter
to the unknown.

Yet it is like the leaf
falling from the tree
caressing us with tenderness.

We are called to
Dance at the sea
Dream in the desert
and sing on the mountains,

So that we can discover ourselves
in a New World
which crumbles old realities
And refused to be Named.

It is a battle cry
yet a song.

Our way of mixing heaven and Earth.

—Sally J. Timmel[69]

The main challenge of our times is to link the inner world of the self with
the outer world of society, and to see both within the larger context of the
material world.

—Dom Helder Camara[70]

There is a certain truth to the expression the dream drives the action. The
greatest contribution we can make to our children is to assist them in their
dreams of a world of pure air and water and sunlight and soil where the
company of living beings would flourish as has not happened in recent years.

—Thomas Berry[71]

Of its very nature it has to unite everything: the world with God; the con-
scious with the unconscious; immersion in its own inwardness with attention
to the course of the world; and purity of mind with a just order of social
relations. Only then will there be a greater awareness of the global signifi-
cance of events; only then will there be greater indignation at abuse of
power; only then will there be a more insatiable thirst for life and freedom.

—Leonardo Boff[72]

A Group Exercise

1. Form a group of three to five people with a mutual interest in a
    particular dream of justice and/or ecology, and compose together

a vision statement of what you trust will be true when Earth and its people are healed and transformed.
2. Create a *mandala* to give visual expression to your statement. Reflect together on what you see, feel, have done, need to know, and still need to do in your area of interest.
3. Develop a concrete action strategy to implement your vision.

Our Experience of Organizing

- What do I want to change?
- How can organization promote the action necessary to bring the change I envision about?

Our Experience of Education

- Recall your early experience of school. Write a paragraph or draw a picture that recaptures that experience.
- How did your experience of education relate to education as described by Freire?

Our Experience of Psychology

- How does your perception of psychology modify your understanding of action?
- Are moral outrage and action for change misplaced internal disturbance or a healthy impulse toward geo-justice? Explain.

Our Experience of Deep Ecology

- Reflect on a time when you remember experiencing a sense of oneness with the natural world.
- In you mind's eye return to that place and reflect on the meaning of the ecological self.
- How do you understand John Seed's statement, "I am the rainforest defending myself"?

Our Experience of Economics

1. Invite members of the group each to think of an item that is overvalued in our culture.

2. Pass out slips of paper and ask the participants to write down the name of the item and draw a symbolic representation of it.
3. Pass a bowl to collect the slips of paper. As the bowl comes to each person, he or she announces the item and shows the symbol before dropping the paper into the bowl.
4. Invite members to think of an item that they feel is undervalued.
5. Pass out slips of paper and ask the participants to write down the name of the item and draw a symbolic representation of it.
6. Again pass a bowl, this time filled with earth. Each person places the strip of paper onto the earth in the bowl, again naming the item and showing the symbol he or she has drawn.
7. Divide the group into smaller working groups (three to five people).
8. Ask each group to prepare and present a news broadcast that focuses on *genuine* indicators of progress related to pollution, resource depletion, and long-term environmental damage.
9. Invite each group to present its report. To close, reflect as an entire group on the process and presentations.

A Group Reflection

1. Present the meaning and purpose of action in achieving language and literacy within and in relationship to the natural world and universe.
2. Present a concrete issue regarding the development of an action strategy.
3. Analyze the action strategy from the perspective of the different groups involved in the action (for example, activists, owners, the natural resource itself).
4. Adapt the principles of the "Council of All Beings" to reflect on this issue; form groups and speak on behalf of the different components of Earth.
5. Close the reflection with a "Talking Circle," in which participants reflect on their experience in doing this exercise.

Process

1. Form groups of three to five people. Ask the question, individually and collectively, "How am I moved to action now?
2. "What action do I feel inspired to take?"

3. "What's keeping me from doing this?"
4. "What are the specific steps and support necessary to move toward the action I am planning to undertake?"

Shared Wisdom—Building a Coalition for Earth

1. What is the focus of your work for the New Creation?.
2. What works for you? Give examples of the competency and skills you have acquired.
3. Where do you feel challenged and invited to grow through your involvement?
4. What are the main issues that have emerged for you and that you are working on at this time?
5. What are the strategies and tactics that you have adapted to accomplish the task?
6. How have you dealt with the problem of language in pondering these questions?
7. Describe what you have learned about yourself, your spirituality, Earth, and the Divine in this process.
8. How has spiritual practice focused and energized your efforts?

Free Beyond All Measure
—*Liberation*

> Our deepest fear is not that we are inadequate. Our deepest fear is that we are powerful beyond measure. It is our light, not our darkness, that most frightens us. We ask ourselves, who am I to be brilliant, gorgeous, talented and fabulous? Actually, who are you not to be? Your playing small does not serve the world. There's nothing enlightened about shrinking so that other people won't feel insecure around you. ... As we let our own light shine, we unconsciously give other people permission to do the same. As we are liberated from our own fear, our presence automatically liberates others.
> —Marianne Williamson[1]

I grew up in Canada, on the shores of the St. Clair River, fifty miles from Detroit—home of Henry Ford and the birthplace of the automobile. Detroit was the archetypal city of the industrial age, the signpost of motors and machines. This proud city stood steadfast, the apex of a worldview that has today lead to disintegration, despair, and decay. How do we restore the Motor City and all Earth? How do we restructure society and achieve a new level of intimacy and relationship with self and others, both humans and the natural world? What is our dream for Earth?

First, we develop a new literacy and share our dreams, and then we tell our stories. Through storytelling, we weave our story into the story of a people. Through organization, popular education, self-discovery, deep ecology, and green economics, we move boldly into meaningful action. When we fully embrace today as a moment of grace, we will discover our destiny as we work toward the freedom and fulfillment of the entire Earth community.

Living at this moment, we are like musicians straining to hear the melody of distant music. As the sound becomes more clear, we take up our part in the great orchestra. Like Thomas Merton, who suddenly, at the corner of 4th and Walnut in Louisville, Kentucky, "awoke from the dream of separateness,"[2] we must deeply realize our interconnectedness with every species and join them in the great work of our time.

Our actions will be designed to meet the needs of those living now without endangering future generations. To do so, we must eradicate from our culture political duplicity, military dominance, the feminization of poverty, environmental racism, and much more. We must restructure society through moral outrage, mutuality, cooperation, interdependence, and economic justice. In this way, we will move toward a cultural boiling point, a moment when the fires of our lives will be ignited by being joined again to the original fire that gave birth to the universe.

Like a cultural chrysalis collapsing, yet unformed, or water that takes the quantum leap to become steam, we are on the verge of a major transition. Change demands sacrifice and courage; we must be ready to invest our energies fully and unconditionally, but not blindly. We will be asked to live in new ways, to:

- develop coalitions of like-minded people;
- live simply with integrity;
- deepen our spiritual practice;
- learn to listen to the universe;
- appreciate beauty and practice patience;
- follow open roads into the future and trust the process;
- embrace our limits; and
- confront cultural pathology wherever it is found.

We stand at the crossroads of either a technocratic or an ecological era. Technology can be put to the service of a more integral Earth community, and so can each of our lives. We either destroy or preserve life. The choice is ours to make.

A New Era for Humanity and Earth

In our communities of hope, we draw on the wisdom of the new science, indigenous peoples, women, and Western Christianity in the context of the world's other great classical traditions. As we awaken to a new consciousness born out of the revelations of science and the experience of the Divine in all creation, we take up the challenge of geo-justice and compassion for Earth.

Our new world view will find its fullest expression as we carry out the historical mission of humanity, the great work of restructuring education, religion, politics, and corporate life while striving to restore Earth and all its species to an era of harmony, balance, and peace. This time of a more mutually enhancing relationship between humanity and creation we call the "ecological age." We are once again inspired by the Civil Rights Movement, the vision of Vatican Council II, and the moral outrage against the war in Vietnam. We relive the pain of the assassinations of so many—John and Robert Kennedy, the Rev. Martin Luther King, Jr., Medgar Evers, Malcolm X. We recall the death of Thomas Merton, the political turmoil of the Democratic Convention. After the collision with the resistant structures of the 1960s, people turned inside, hoping to change themselves when they found the structures slow to change. Therapies of many kinds flourished. Arthur Janov's *Primal Scream* became popular. Charles Reich's *Greening of America* became a handbook for the back-to-the-land movement. Communes proliferated as people strove to heal the alienation of urban life. The mass exodus of professional religious in the 1960s was followed by the silent leaving of men and women who were fifty or sixty years of age. Liberation movements flourished in Latin America and Africa, while a renaissance of community organizing spread to many major cities in North America. Paulo Freire's *Pedagogy of the Oppressed* became known around the world. (Freire's later work *Pedagogy of Hope* looks back on those days.)

Indeed, history has much to teach us. The discoveries of new science, the awareness of the ecological crisis, feminism, the capacity to read the scriptures of the natural world, growing awareness of interior experience, and cultural history have become signposts that help us move from the past into the future with hope. This new hope inspires us to confront the crises of a mechanistic and destructive society and move forward with greater awareness and solidarity.

The conviction that experience is more important than ideas was well stated by Gregory Bateson, author of *Ecology of the Mind,* who suggested that we should refrain from eating the menu rather than the meal. Mythologist Joseph Campbell further emphasized this perspective, pointing out that when we say we are seeking meaning in our lives, we are really seeking the experience of being alive. That experience takes place at its deepest level when there is a resonance between our innermost being and our outer world.

I believe that we, as a species, are called to invent a culture that is congruent with our worldview. Ants build anthills wherever they are, and bees build beehives; they are genetically coded to do so. As humans with self-reflexive consciousness, we need to foster a culture that is mutually enhancing with Earth. We need to abandon a culture that is mechanistic and separate and begin again to fashion rituals, dreams, stories, actions, and art that are congruent with and flow out of the new story that we, as a people, are just beginning to tell.

During an event at the Cathedral of John the Divine in New York City, Thomas Berry remarked, "The universe is shouting at us; it wants the artists to shout back." My conviction is that we are *all* invited to shout back. We are called to shout back as artists of the new culture, attuned to the new living cosmology being written about, researched, and lived out in our time. This moment is drawing us ever closer to a collective awareness of how our lives could be.

In my chemistry class in high school, we were taught to put crystals into a flask until the solution became supersaturated. Each person striving to live out of the new cosmology and consciousness is adding his or her "crystals" to the flask of global awareness. In this way, we participate in the transformation of consciousness and culture necessary to move us forward as a new people on a new Earth. The courage necessary to accomplish this task is described in the words of paleontologist and theologian Teilhard de Chardin: "At each step of descent a new person was disclosed within me. . . . And when I had to stop my exploration because the path faded beneath my steps, I found a bottomless abyss at my feet and out of it came arising I know not from where . . . the current which I love to call my life."[3] This movement into a living cosmology will not be without a price. It requires fresh energy to ignite this divine epiphany in our lives. It requires that we break down the armoring of the heart and break through into healing action for Earth and its people.

A scene from the drama of "Bernstein's Mass" comes to mind. When the celebrant dropped the crystal chalice on the sanctuary floor, it broke into many, many pieces, each an expression of beauty and brokenness. In a similar way, each of us as a vessel of the future is a thread of the fabric of interconnectedness. Like iron filings drawn together by a magnet, we are being drawn together to give birth to a way of living on a planet at peace. In our search for healing and wholeness, we are simultaneously mothers, midwives, and children of the ecological era that awaits us. Our task is to extend the capacity for relationship toward the entire Earth community. As Thomas Merton reminds us,

Then it was as if I suddenly saw the secret beauty of their hearts; the depths of their hearts where neither desire nor self-knowledge can reach the person that each one is in God's eyes. If only they could all see themselves as they really are. If only we could see each other that way all the time there would be no more war, no more hatred, no more cruelty, and no more greed.[4]

Or yet again, in the words of the Rev. Martin Luther King, Jr., "All people are caught in an inescapable network of mutuality, tied in a single garment of destiny."[5]

Entering the ecological age involves a transformation of alienation into connectedness, conformity into uniqueness, and autism into awareness as we fashion new dreams, stories, and actions to bring us forward. In a very real way, our task is to live the future that already exists, the already but not yet Kingdom of God. This task and challenge involves a profound shift in consciousness and worldview. It means seeing the world differently and acting differently.

Our action must inevitably be on the side of the oppressed; it must challenge the status quo rather than sacralize it and foster new relationships to ensure common energy for a common good. The result of this effort will be a revitalization of sacred and significant proportion. Liberation happens in three ways: we are freed from structures of oppression; we experience personal transformation; and we achieve fulfillment in our relationship to the divine. In each action for liberation of the human-Earth community, these components must be present.

- There is a local response to a particular need. This rescues us from abstraction and engages us in the here-and-now realities of life.
- We are involved in face-to-face contact in real relationships and in a common cause fostered by our human interaction and our concern for Earth.
- Central to our efforts and a basis for our work is the building of bioregional communities to provide support for people. Members come together to tell stories, reflect on their actions, assess their attitudes to Earth, and plan better ways of being. These gatherings overflow into liturgical celebrations, where people connect their experience with what they most deeply believe and their compassion for Earth. These attitudes toward Earth are manifested by healthier and more ecological lifestyles. These base communities then become the framework for action that is initiated on both the local and global level to bring about changes that support more integral relationships between Earth and all its people, actions fostered by a passion and compassion for Earth.
- In almost every case, we will desire to engage in global networking and the building of structures to overcome forces of destruction. And we will celebrate peoples' creativity in order to bring about structural change.

We will be energized by beliefs that support actions for radical social and ecological transformation, actions that will cleanse Earth from "toxins of domination." We will create a sacred space that is nourished by insight, information, and challenge. Fueled by the gift of being able to express ourselves without interruption or censure, we will experience the transition from oppression and defiance to empowerment and hope. Drawing on the resources of imagination and compassion, we will keep our dreams alive as we learn how to live them.

Through participating in a partnership of shared struggle, truth telling, and a bold moral vision, our actions will redeem the soul of our culture. We will work toward a heightened experience of community, communion, and a common bond. We will put behind us the culture in which a child asked, as he walked in his neighborhood in Washington, DC, "Was there a war here?"

We need to declare to the youth of every nation that peace is possible, a peace that brings all life to fruition and celebrates the well-being of Earth. This came home to me at a ritual in 1995 marking the fiftieth anniversary of the founding of the United Nations. One hundred fifty students from many of the countries of the world participated. Each one approached a large bowl carried a flask of water from his or her country. Pouring the water into a large bowl, each student proclaimed, "This is the sacred water from [name of country]." This simple action was a powerful proclamation of the possibility of global peace. The bowl became the container of waters from many countries, a common vessel, a powerful symbol of the coming together necessary for a planetary peace.

Today small groups on the edge of the dominant culture, particularly those who are experiencing the stress of our pathological society, are attuned to the possibilities that this movement provides and are committed to undertake the great task of being aligned to the dynamics of Earth. Indeed, we must be willing to face our fear, transcend our denial of the pervasive misery of our times, and take up the task of living fully and embracing the entire Earth community. This awesome task makes possible the ecological age:

• experiencing kinship with every creature;
• being challenged, stretched, and fully expressive;
• being totally attuned to an individual or group so that personal energy, group energy, and the universe's energy are felt as one;
• participating with others in moments of ecstasy, breakthrough, and fulfillment;

- entering into a profound comprehension of the cosmic context of our lives;
- living in a world of wonder and possibility;
- connecting with others and Earth at the deepest level;
- experiencing self, other, and Earth as integral, noble, and whole;
- becoming people who generate order and complexity in the universe; and
- living into new possibilities through the experience of truth, energy, and purpose.

This is the future that beckons—uncertain yet exciting and open. It is ours to create. We will begin to act in a manner that is congruent with how we experience the world (Earth literacy); that is true to our vision and how we see the future (dream); that is attuned to who we are and the unfolding of our lives within the context of Earth and the universe (story); that moves all creation to an era of peace and harmony (action); that is creative and transformative for all affected and mutually enhancing within the larger Earth community (liberation).

The poet Mary Oliver presents us with an important question: "What do we do with our wild and precious lives?"[6]

Origins and Roots

The new story, a spirituality of Earth and geo-justice, shatters our previous perceptions and experiences. Suddenly, we are presented with enormous new challenges with profound implications for the future of our planet.

Flooded with new energy, we feel a growing affinity for the mystery and meaning being revealed to us. Everything becomes revelatory: cricket, ant, tree, and human are each a "book" about God. The incarnation is ever present among us; birth continues, flowers bloom, puppies are born, morning comes, ideas and projects are brought into existence. Bethlehem encompasses us in a multitude of ways.

Differentiation, the source of creativity and resurrection, is an expression of the creator God; diversity astonishes us with beauty, blessings, and new life. We make our Easter with Earth and every species.

Interiority indicates the source of origins and story and the locus of the Word of God. This place of depth, the grand canyon of our souls, reflects the capacity of our interior experience to be coextensive with the universe itself. Where pain resides, letting go happens and death has meaning. We rediscover a cosmic crucifixion in the death of the rain forest, the reduction of the ozone layer, domestic violence, substance abuse, and the accelerated extinction of species.

Communion points toward interconnectedness and the divine Spirit from which transformation comes. This is energy that weaves together the seamless garment of social and ecological concerns into a blanket of balance and tapestry of geo-justice, the source of a planetary pentecost from which will flow harmony and peace. When these principles of the universe are present, the Trinity is palpable among us, and the Divine is present in our midst.

Poised at the precipice of the new millennium, we are experiencing an Exodus moment; we are leaving behind an era of human pathos and ecological devastation and moving forward to embrace a new era of beauty, enhancement, and health, a new revelatory moment.

We know that our dreams originate in the imagination and are the starting point of hope. With this in mind, we move forward toward a freedom and fulfillment that is guided and fostered by the visions that spring forth from the recesses of our souls.

Astonished by our dreams and enchanted by our story, within this new context, we focus our prophetic acts as expressions of the pulsating heart of the universe. These acts of re-creation evoke in us a realization that we are attuned to the lyrics of creation and are, in fact, articulating a language for the music of the universe.

Ultimately, freedom and fulfillment for the human lies in celebration such as remembering those ecstatic moments when a sunset, a bird song, a family meal, a snowcapped mountain, sunrise over a pond, a river, a meadow, or a night sky have quenched our thirst for wonder and liberated our hearts.

This is our challenge, our privilege, and our call—to sing our unique line in the lyrics for re-creation. The following words are composed in lyrical language as music for the universe and a promise of the new creation we are called to create.

A Canticle for Re-Creation

Lyrics for Re-Creation is the word written for the music of creation, the
    language of freedom and fulfillment resonating from the heart of
    the universe.
    the orchestration of Earth literacy, dream, story, action, and libera-
    tion from within the symphony of life.

Lyrics for Re-Creation is for all who feel the fever of the new millennium,
     all who are ready to lament the pain of a devastated Earth,
     all who would reclaim the soul of our country and culture,
     all the wise and compassionate ones who have gone before and
     those in our midst.

Lyrics for Re-Creation rescues us from a pathology enveloped in practices
     of addiction, greed, prejudice, and repression,
     liberates us from separateness, alienation, and being alone, invites
     us into oneness with ecology, universe, and home.

Lyrics for Re-Creation sees life and Earth as sacred,
     inspires us to stand in intimate awe of the depth, beauty, and differ-
     ence in all that is,
     encourages us to embrace each revelatory moment in the natural
     world,
     challenges us to restore Earth to its pristine beauty and restructure
     society to eliminate oppression,
     asks that we reduce the negative impact of the human and liberate
     creation through a more mutually enhancing relationship between
     humans and Earth.

Lyrics for Re-Creation fosters our dreams
     as we stand at the feet of raped rain forests, urban decay, and civil
     wars,
     as we listen for prophetic voices and envision a planet at peace in
     an ecological age that fosters communion, acknowledges diversity
     and celebrates spontaneity.

Lyrics for Re-Creation is about the story of the universe, the
     evolutionary, self-generating, organic process that reveals our cos-
     mic place, and
     about our story, an unfolding narrative out of which strategies and
     strengths boil into actions for Earth.

Lyrics for Re-Creation fashions a coalition for Earth from
     organization, education, self-discovery, deep ecology and green eco-
     nomics, and
     reminds us that literacy, dream, story, and action culminate in libera-
     tion, the freedom and fulfillment of every species.

Lyrics for Re-Creation calls us to celebrate the intimacy of life,
     to energize our hearts with hope,

to proclaim an unfolding path of trust
to initiate a dance of freedom for Earth.

Lyrics for Re-Creation invites us to befriend our gorgeous planet
from the grandeur of the Andes in Bolivia to the azure beauty of
Lake Louise in Canada,
from the corn fields of Nebraska to the rice fields of China.

Lyrics for Re-Creation extends our understanding of the God of
history to One who permeates the natural world, from the struggle
for freedom in Peru to the challenge for pure water in the Great
Lakes.

Lyrics for Re-Creation will keep hope in mind as we celebrate the
green shoots breaking through the blacktop of an ending era, as
we await a new cultural wave gathering and bursting forth on the
shore of life.

Lyrics for Re-Creation celebrates the great symphony of life that
dreams of a future for our children, and
gives voice to stories told in barrios, townships, ghettos, and com-
munities of hope.

Toward Liberating Action

- Share in writing and conversation your understanding and experience
  of Earth literacy.
- Reflect on your dream of how you would like your life to be. Share
  your reflections with another person or group.
- Reveal your story by drawing an image and writing an accompanying
  statement. Share this description of your story with an individual or
  group.
- Gather a working group (three to five people) and develop the action
  steps necessary to move toward liberation on a personal, public, and
  planetary level.

FOR REFLECTION

"Creation is the first act of earth literacy.
Earth literacy is the first act of the dream.
The dream is the first act of storytelling.
The story is the beginning of action.
Action is the first act of liberation.
Literacy, dream, and story are actions for the liberation of all creation."

Epilogue
—Soulwork for the New Millennium

Yesterday is already a dream
And tomorrow is only a vision
But today well lived
Makes every yesterday a dream of happiness
And every tomorrow
A vision of hope.

—from Sanskrit[1]

We gathered as a group to explore how the crises of nature, culture, and soul impinged upon our lives. An elementary school teacher spoke eloquently for the children, saying, "They are in crisis: they are lost and angry; no one loves them." A corporate executive lamented the loneliness and disconnection in her life and the lives of the people she knew. An artist proclaimed the pain of feeling separate, the sadness of being cut off from nature and self. A business woman mourned the report of an eleven-year-old boy who shot another child and was killed himself. A chaplain for youth offenders discussed the despair and lost sense of beauty and reverence in the lives of the incarcerated youth with whom he worked. A mother with a child in prison proclaimed the crisis in our culture; she described the breakdown of family, religion, and home. A member of the religious community described the homeless plight of urban refugees and mused about her own search for a home. A missionary revealed his perception of the "lack of communion," the unwillingness to share and distribute life's resources; he insightfully pointed out that our jobs are subsidized by the poor. An artist talked about the polluted ocean near his home and the homeless people on the streets. Someone spoke of the shame of being an "ugly American" while multinational corporations ravage Third-World peoples. A young woman from the southern United States mourned the extinction of species and the loss of wisdom. A woman from Northern Ireland described the tragedy there and celebrated the truce recently announced, a moment of hope rising from decades of despair, this "deficit of soul."

In the face of these crises, we are called to be healed of our autism and sensitized to the beauty of this planet. Faced with the influence of an anthropocentric culture, where humans see themselves as separate and superior, we challenge soulless corporate giants like Exxon, which polluted the waters of Prince William Sound; and all the individuals and corporations that encourage the exploitation of nature for human purposes, whether by clearcutting the redwoods of Northern California or pumping pesticides into the potatoes of Prince Edward Island. In this "dark night" of our culture, our task is to overcome what James Joyce called "moral suffocation" and extend the sense of soul to the entire Earth community.

As we shift from a deistic, mechanical God to an immanent, sacred, enveloping presence, we put "the photon back in the Incarnation."[2] Through the synthesis of ancient wisdom and modern science, we understand, experience, and express a vision and a practice that is evolutionary and just.

The ecological revolution is pointing us toward a new sense of the sacred. We are challenged to see the world in a new way, to become new humans on a new Earth; from this perspective, we develop actions to liberate Earth and its peoples. We work to bring about a new cultural coding for these beginning moments of the ecological age. As Miriam Therese MacGillis says, "If we can redefine our perspective on self to include the self of Earth and the universe's self, then we have a whole new level of insight and energy to help us through our contemporary crisis into a new stage of our own development as a human community."[3] With science and intuition as our guides, we plumb the frontiers of inner and outer space and strive to translate our new knowing into new living.

Whether we are a teachers in the inner city or a missionaries in Mindanao, Philippines, our task is to join forces with the deeper energies of the planet. We do this by nurturing the children, healing loneliness, building community, responding to pain, and celebrating interconnectedness. We embrace the challenge of the new millennium as a people who strain to hear a distant melody. As the music becomes more clear, we begin to write the lyrics for the music that is the harmony of the ecological age that awaits us. The melody of this sacred moment calls for a new integration between humans and the natural world; it calls us to a "richly elaborated life, connected to society and nature . . . woven into the culture of family, nation and globe."[64]

There is no prototype or model for the future; what lies before us is an invitation to participate in a new network of mutuality.

- Convinced that a preferential option for Earth will liberate the people and the planet, we strive to transform this time of madness into a moment of reciprocity and peace.
- Standing at this threshold of newness, we pledge our energies to make a better world for children, the newborn of every species.
- Our vision of freedom and fulfillment finds its source within the recesses of our cultural soul, and its full expression in this cradle of creativity we know as Earth.
- Following our dream into action, we realize our destiny and call.
- Fueled by hope and compassion, we give expression to interdependence in every aspect of our lives.
- We liberate the imagination of presuppositions of pathology and pain and celebrate differentiation, interiority, and communion as the pattern of the culture we are called to create.
- Freed from exile on our planet, we enter the promised land of liberation as we come home to the cosmos, people, and ourselves.
- Re-energized for life, we begin to create a new future marked by peace among nations, races, genders, cities, humans and the natural world—a peace that will liberate Earth and bring freedom and fulfillment to all.

A Canticle for the New Creation

Called forth by wisdom's crises
We edge unknowingly
To the precipice of our era and our time.

Summoned by music, melody and you,
With lyrical language
We celebrate new options for our day,
And collectively decide
To return to our origins and begin again.

Here in this moment of literacy for life
This time of dream and depth
We are called to reinvent our story and ourselves,
At this action time
Here on the threshold of freedom, and new beginnings.

Appendices

A. Action Autobiography
B. I Have a Dream . . .
C. Project Earth
D. Processes for Re-Creation

A.   Action Autobiography

The following are from my own action autobiography.

What is your earliest recollection of an action through which you tried to bring about change?
When I was eleven, I made a deal with my baseball manager that during games that my brother pitched, I would catch. The other catcher on the team was older and better than I was, but my "deal" ensured that I would be able to play regularly.

How was this action a statement of hope and courage and a confrontation with resignation and inertia?
It took courage for me to try to change the system (which decreed that the better player always would play), so I could obtain something that was important to me. It is also true that I felt somewhat ambivalent about my success, because I was not the better player.

How did your action result in increased solidarity with others?
My action increased my solidarity with my brother and with some of our teammates, because we saw that together we could influence some of the conditions under which we played.

Did this action increase your belief in people as a source of action on behalf of freedom, equality, and peace?
While this action was my introduction to influencing power and creating change, I was still operating as an eleven-year-old child. From the perspective of values, my action left a lot to be desired in terms of freedom, fairness, and peace.

What people bring you hope, promote freedom, and model courage and compassion?
There are people who support my efforts and believe in me. Among them are Jack Egan, David Steindl-Rast, Tom Berry, and my brother and sister. . . . I would also include as models certain political leaders,

such as Clinton, Gore, Aristide, and Haval, and moral leaders, including Dan Berrigan and Dom Helder Camara. There are also others, pastoral women and men of great faith and prophetic courage, who inspire me.

How are you engaged with the forces of oppression, the symbols and sources of limitations in your life?

I experience the forces of oppression in structures: ecclesiastic, academic, and political. I experience these in my personal struggles against fear, despair, and internalized oppression and in my confrontations with a heart often broken and a mind sometimes divided.

What has been your most prophetic effort on behalf of Earth?

When I think of my efforts for Earth, I become mindful of the initiatives that have engaged people's efforts, that have been marked with continuity, and whose long-term impact is difficult to measure: a halfway house in London, Ontario, Canada; a center for children, seniors, and the homeless in Sarnia, Ontario, Canada; a project for friends and associates of former mental patients in Toronto; a newspaper, *Catholic New Times;* the Institute for Christian Life; the Canadian Caucus for Theological Field Education; Regional Connectors in Creation Spirituality; Project Earth; the birth of the Sophia Center and my published works: *Geo-Justice—A Preferential Option for Earth, Earth Story, Sacred Story,* and *Lyrics for Re-Creation: Language for the Music of the Universe.*

What universal principles do you believe in and how do they serve to guide your work?

I am increasingly aware that the ethics of the cósmos must guide my life. The principles of differentiation, interiority, and communion are central to my values. I see that the work of human rights and dignity is central to the recognizing and honoring diversity. Listening enhances my capacity for relationships and reflects the interiority of life. Finally, the capacity for knowing compassion and interconnectedness is central to my life and future work. Together these principles share a trinitarian perspective that provides the framework for my life and work.

Other questions that form part of my action autobiography, and may be useful to others, follow.

In what ways have you worked toward unity between your awareness of the new cosmology and your actions for Earth?

What have you learned about yourself and Earth through your efforts?

What continues to hold you back?

What have you seen, felt, or done (or intend to do) to increase your capacity to bring about change?

How have your efforts toward freedom deepened your experience of the divine?

What do you want to create on behalf of Earth in the next phase of your journey?

What do you need to learn in order to foster your awareness of Earth?

What components of geo-justice and creation spirituality inform your vision of the future?

B.   I Have a Dream . . .

. . . that out of the ecological devastation in our contemporary culture, we will find a cosmic focus for our time;

. . . that within the context of political aggression and moral imperialism, people of all lands will become instruments of global harmony and peace;

. . . that in the face of escapism and despair, the entire Earth community will find hope and inspiration;

. . . that confronted with consumerism, propaganda, and drugs, we will reach for a spirituality of liberation and creation to resolve our dividedness and enable us to become whole, rooted, and secure with Earth and all its species;

. . . that when we are overwhelmed by unemployment, poverty, and meaninglessness, we will work toward sustainable development, employment, and healthy food;

. . . that when faced with the attachments of narcissism and greed, each global citizen will respond with generosity and love to foster and protect Earth;

. . . that when faced with futility, anonymity, and despair, people will find resonance in the wisdom of the past and encouragement through the innovations of today;

. . . that when bombarded with popular notions of burnout, repression, and loss, the people of Earth will channel their creative energies into life-giving projects of courage and compassion;

. . . that at this time of metaphysical sameness and repressed uniqueness, each person and species will celebrate a preferential option for other *as* other;

. . . that within a context of exploitation, disenchantment, and lost dignity, women and men of every land will rediscover their integrity and purpose;

. . . that in a culture of aimlessness and undiscovered paths, all children will discover their vision and particular contribution to Earth; and

. . . that in the search for meaning, purpose, and the experience of delight, all global citizens will become more profoundly in touch with their own magnificence, open to letting go of whatever holds

them back, and disposed to the transformation of society and self
by imaginative responses to love.

FOR REFLECTION

A shot rings out in Memphis
And is heard around the world
As will the dream continue
Becomes our question for today.

His vision lives among us
As history takes a turn
Toward human rights and justice
For the voiceless in us all.

Mantin is a prophet
Showing forth the way
That each of us can honor
In the context of the day.

His voice and dream continue
To echo in our hearts
Drawing forth fresh wisdom
For the renewal of our lives.

As we resonate with courage
And conviction from within
To heal the pain and pressure
Of the ache that yet remains.

Yes, his soul remains among us
And his dream still shows the way
For his hope lives on among us
To illuminate our day.

C. Project Earth
—A Center for Cultural Rebirth and Geo-Justice

Project Earth can be described as a center created to respond to the magnitude of ecological and cultural change taking place at this moment in history. Its purpose is to mediate the insights of science, art, politics, and spiritual practice in and through individuals and institutions—educational, church, and public—who are striving to understand, interpret, and promote the emerging consciousness for Earth literacy.

Project Earth will benefit the entire Earth community by fostering a reverence for diversity and interconnectedness among youth, racial minorities, the economically oppressed, men and women. The project will proved information and support for those individuals and groups who have taken up the task of translating the wisdom of a new holistic world view (a living cosmology) through approaches and practices aligned to bring peace among peoples and integrity to all of creation.

Project Earth is designed to make available in an organized fashion— through written and recorded resources—the cultural implications of this new convergence of science, art, politics, and spiritual practice. It will discover, through research and action, an appropriate infrastructure to provide information, support, and the possibility of a common action to heal the alienation between people and Earth. This new center will synthesize diverse approaches that are being developed around the world—South Africa, Latin America, Canada, and the United States. This collective wisdom will be available to the ever-expanding constituency of those whose work for justice is rooted in a compassionate respect for Earth.

Project Earth will draw on the practice articulated by James Conlon in *Geo-Justice: A Preferential Option for Earth* and *Earth Story, Sacred Story* and *Lyrics for Re-Creation: Language for the Music of the Universe,* as well as parallel sources including *The Universe Story* by Brian Swimme and Thomas Berry, *The Dream of Earth* by Thomas Berry, *A Theology of Liberation* by Gustavo Gutiérrez, *God in South Africa* by Albert Nolan, and *Ecology and Liberation* by Leonardo Boff.

Project Earth will mediate the meaning of the new cosmology as revealed in the sacred story of the universe by reflecting on its personal and cultural implications. It will provide:

• workshops and seminars;
• periodicals, books, and recorded resources;
• communication among an ever-expanding network;
• development of practical projects from both a global and local perspective;
• collegiality with like-minded groups;
• transformative avenues for reflection and change; and
• a response to emerging needs.
• For information, Lectures and Workshops, please write to Jim Conlon care of Project Earth.

Project Earth, % *Center for the New Millennium, Suite 296, 1678 Shattuck Avenue, Berkeley CA 94709*

D. Processes for Re-Creation

Stories of Intimate Connections with the Natural World

1. Give an image of the natural world to each person.
2. Invite the participants to respond to the images.
3. When they have discovered who or what they are, invite them to relate their experience of being an expression of the natural world.

Finding Our Focus

1. Describe a *mandala* (any of various designs symbolic of the universe).
2. Give each participant with a sheet of paper with a circle drawn on it. The center of the circle should be marked.
3. Invite the participants to draw or write on the paper, creating mandala that expresses their own questions and impulses to creativity.
4. Invite each person to present his or her mandala to the group.

Coding the Culture

1. Review the term *New Story* and describe briefly the three principles of differentiation, interiority, and communion.
2. Develop the geo-justice connections: local (differentiation); psychosocial (interiority); and global (communion).
3. Invite the participants to draw and write about the component they feel most passionate about.
4. Ask participants to find like-minded people and form a group.
5. After allowing time for the small groups to discuss the principles further, bring their reflections to the total group.

Listening to the Stone (outdoor activity)

1. Gather the group and instruct the participants to find a stone with which they have a special connection.
2. After five minutes, gather again. Ask each participant to share with the group what he or she learned from this stone.
3. After each person speaks, have him or her approach a designated "sacred space" and place the stone there and light a candle.
4. When everyone has spoken, conclude with a song.

Eco-Milling (developed from the work of Joanna Macy)

1. Form a group of four and explore how you are moved to action at this critical moment of history.
2. Ask what action the group feels inspired to take now.
3. Investigate what is keeping you from doing this.
4. What are the specific steps and support necessary to move toward this action that you are hoping to undertake?

The Cosmic Walk (An Alternative Approach)

Prepare a calibrated rope marked according to the events named below. Coil the rope in a spiral. Place a candle and a placard naming each event. In turn, participants step into the spiral, light a candle by the placard and proclaim the event. When all candles are lit, each person steps into the spiral and moves from the center outward, observing the events of the universe. When each exits the spiral, he or she declare, "The universe celebrates (name)" and is welcomed by the group. This ritual was developed by Sr. Miriam Therese MacGillis of Genesis Farm.

The New Story

15 billion years ago	The universe came into being
5 billion years ago	The solar system and Earth emerged
3 billion years ago	Life emerged as simple bacteria
2 billion years ago	Oxygen formed in the atmosphere
1 billion years ago	Earth reproduced life sexually

800 million years ago	Multicellular life emerged
520 million years ago	The first fish emerged
420 million years ago	The first land plants appeared
360 million years ago	The first insects came to be
220 million years ago	The first mammals emerged
180 million years ago	The first birds took flight
130 million years ago	The first flowering plants appeared
65 million years ago	Dinosaurs became extinct
5 million years ago	The Ice Age occurred
100 thousand years ago	*Homo sapiens* emerged
10 thousand years ago	Agriculture began
7 thousand years ago	Abraham and Sarah left Ur
2 thousand years ago	Jesus of Nazareth was born
1 hundred years ago	The first photograph was created
57 years ago	The atom was split
28 years ago	The first human stepped on the Moon
7 years ago	The wall between East and West disintegrated
Today	The universe dreams us forth by name

The Cosmic Walk—Expanded

1. Create the spiral with moments of unfolding from the original fireball until today (see above).
2. Invite each participant to step into the spiral with an article that reveals an aspect of who he or she is. (Each person places the object at the center, beside the fireball, and then exits.)
3. With instrumental music playing, have each person enter the spiral from the outside, walk to the center, ring a bell, light a candle, and retrieve the item he or she placed there.
4. As each exits the spiral, he or she says aloud: *What do I want to create?*

The Spiritual Narrative—From Dream to Action

I. Process
   A. Form groups of three to five people.
   B. Meet periodically during preparation and development of your spiritual narrative.

     C.   Prepare an approach for sharing your personal and group story with the larger group.

II. Focus

     A.   *Personal:* Name moments of beauty, hope, pain, interia, break-through, birth, interconnectedness and compassion in your life.

     B.   *Bioregional:* What are your memories, experiences, and percep-tions of the natural world that have been "moments of grace" and marked your relationship to Earth?

     C.   *Cultural:* How have the trends and countertrends of the culture shaped your sense of the sacred through language and imagi-nation (images, art, movements, heroes, heroines, music, media, politics, etc.)?

     D.   *Cosmic:* In what way do you understand your story to be a paragraph in the Universe story? How have your life experi-ences been formed in the same "primordial furnace"? How have personal and cultural transformations paralleled the cos-mic transformations of the universe (that is, Galactic Story, Earth Story, Life on Earth Story, Human Story)?

          Describe how the three principles that emerge from the story (differentiation, interiority, and communion) have formed and focused your story.

III. Sharing: Prepare your story and present it in any format (music, movement, painting, poetry, prose, video, etc.)

Acts of Re-Creation

- What is the earliest recollection you have of initiating change for Earth and its people? Describe.
- Reflect on the following questions: "How am I moved to action now?" "In what way is my action a declaration of hope, courage, and solidarity with the entire Earth community?"
- As you ponder options for action, how do you experience the inspira-tion to act? What keeps you from acting?
- What role does coalition-building play regarding your engagement in action?
- How does your response to the question, "What do I want to create?", shape your action strategies as you ponder the next phase of your life?
- How does making a preferential option for Earth affect your actions in the world? How has taking action been an occasion of self-discovery

in your life? What have you learned about yourself; about Earth about the Divine?

- Does your impulse toward action include protecting the natural world and the rhythms of the planet where you live (your bioregion)?
- Who are the people and movements who encourage you in your journey into action?
- How does your experience of the Divine and your spiritual practice fuel your action in the world?
- What are the possibilities for common action in your life? Who are your allies in these efforts?
- How do you want to be remembered for the actions you have taken? In what way do you desire that your action take place outside of existing structures?
- What has been your most prophetic act on behalf of Earth?
- What have you felt, done, or intend to do to increase your capacity to act?
- What actions do you intend to engage in in the next phase of your journey?

Bibliography

Abrams, Jeremiah, ed. *The Shadow in America: Reclaiming the Soul of a Nation*. Novato, CA: Natari Publishing, 1994.

Aldredge-Clanton, Jann. *In Search of the Christ–Sophia*. Mystic, CT: Twenty-Third Publications, 1996.

Alinsky, Saul. *Rules for Radicals*. New York: Random House, 1971.

———. *Reveille for Radicals*. New York: Vintage Books, 1969.

Babin, Pierre, and Mercedes Iannone. *The New Era in Religious Communication*. Minneapolis: Augsburg Fortress Press, 1991.

Batstone, David, ed. *New Visions for the Americas: Religious Engagement and Social Transformation*, Minneapolis: Augsburg Fortress Press, 1993.

Baum, Gregory. *Man Becoming—God in Secular Experience*. Garden City, NY: Herder & Herder, 1971.

Bellah, Robert, Richard Marsden, William Sullivan, Ann Swidler, and Steven Tipton. *The Good Society*. New York: Alfred Knopf, 1991.

Berry, James. "Circular 191." Raleigh, NC: The Center for Reflection on the Second Law, May 1991.

Berry, Thomas, and Brian Swimme. *The Universe Story*. San Francisco: Harper San Francisco 1992.

Berry, Thomas. *Creative Energy: Bearing Witness for Earth*. San Francisco: Sierra Club–Pathstone, 1988, 1996.

———. "The Ecozoic Era." E. F. Schumacher Society Lectures. October 1991.

———. *The Dream of Earth*. San Francisco: Sierra Club Books, 1988.

———. "*Riverdale Papers*." Unpublished manuscript.

Boff, Leonardo. *Ecology and Liberation—A New Paradigm*. Maryknoll, NY: Orbis Books, 1995.

Colleran, P. K., ed. *Walking with Contemplation*. Berkeley: Cath Foundation, 1983.

Conlon, James. *Earth Story, Sacred Story*. Mystic, CT: Twenty-Third Publications, 1994.

———. *Geo-Justice: A Preferential Option for Earth*. Woodlake Books, Winfield, B.C., Canada; San Jose, CA: Resource Publications, 1990.

Cousineau, Phil, ed. *Soul—An Archeology*. San Francisco: Harper San Francisco, 1994.

Dyer, George J., ed. *An American Catholic Catechism*, San Francisco: Harper & Row, 1975.

Edwards, Dennis. *Jesus the Wisdom of God—An Ecological Theology*. Maryknoll, NY: Orbis Books, 1995.

Finks, P. David. *The Radical Vision of Saul Alinsky*. Mahwah, NJ: Paulist Press, 1984.

Forest, Jim. *Love is the Measure: A Bibliography of Dorothy Day*. Maryknoll, NY: Orbis Books, 1994.

Fowler, James. *Weaving the New Creation*. San Francisco: Harper San Francisco, 1991.

Fowler, Robert Booth. *The Greening of Protestant Thought*. Chapel Hill, NC: University of North Carolina Press, 1995.

Fox, Matthew. *Meditations with Meister Eckhart*. Santa Fe, NM; Bear & Co., 1982.

Fox, Warwich. *Toward a Transpersonal Ecology*. Boston: Shambhala, 1992.

Fragomeni, Richard and John Pawlikowski, eds. *The Ecological Challenge*, Collegeville, MN: Liturgical Press, 1994.

Freire, Paulo. *Education for Critical Consciousness*. New York: Seabury Press, 1973.

———. *Pedagogy of the City*. New York: Continuum, 1993.

———. *Pedagogy of the Oppressed*. New York: Seabury Press, 1970.

———. *Pedagogy of Hope: Reliving the Pedagogy of the Oppressed*. New York: Continuum, 1989.

———. "Seminar on Community Education and Development." Toronto: Institute for Studies in Education, University of Toronto, 1976.

———. *Letters to Christina—Reflections on My Life's Work*. New York: Routledge, 1996.

Fritz, Robert. *The Path of Least Resistance*. New York: Fawcett Columbine, 1989.

Gerzon, Mark. *A House Divided: Six Belief System Struggles for America's Soul*. New York: G. B. Putnam's Sons, 1996.

Gore, Albert. *Earth in the Balance*. Boston: Houghton Mifflin, 1992.

Granberg, Wesley. *Redeeming the Creation—The Rio Earth Summit*. MichaelsonRisk Book Series, Geneva: World Council of Churches Publications, 1992.

Green, Clifford, ed. *Churches, Cities and Human Community: Urban Ministry in the United States, 1945–1985*. Grand Rapids, MI: William Ferdmans Publishing, 1996.

Green, Lorna. *Earth Age—A New Vision of God, the Human and Earth.* Mahwah, NJ: Paulist Press, 1994.

Griffiths, Bede. *A New Vision of Reality.* Springfield, IL: Templegate Publishers, 1989.

Grof, Stanislav, with Hal Bennett. *The Holotropic Mind.* San Francisco: Harper San Francisco, 1990.

Gutiérrez, Gustavo. *We Drink from Our Own Wells.* Maryknoll, NY: Orbis Books, 1984.

———. *The Theology of Liberation.* Maryknoll, NY: Orbis Books, 1988.

Hahn, Thich Nhut. *Be Still and Know.* New York: Riverhead Books, 1996.

Hallman, David, ed. *Voices from South and North.* Geneva: World Council of Churches Publications, and Maryknoll, NY: Orbis Books, 1994.

Harte, John. *The Green Fuse—An Ecological Odyssey.* Berkeley: University of California Press, 1993.

Havel, Vaclav. Reprint. El Sobrate, CA: SIS Institute, Spring 1994.

Hayden, Tom. *The Lost Gospel of the Earth.* San Francisco: Sierra Club Books, 1996.

Hayes, Edward. *Prayers for a Planetary Pilgrim.* Easton, KS: Forest of Peace Books, 1989.

Heffern, Richard. *Adventures in Simple Living.* Easton, KS; Forest of Peace, 1996.

Hennelly, Alfred T., S.J., ed. *Santo Domingo and Beyond: Documents and Commentaries from the Historic Meeting of the Latin American Bishops Conference.* Maryknoll, NY: Orbis Books, 1993.

———. *Liberation Theologies: The Global Pursuit of Justice.* Mystic, CT: Twenty-Third Publication, 1995.

Hessel, Dieter, ed. *After Nature's Revolt: Eco-Justice and Theology.* Minneapolis: Augsburg Fortress Press, 1992.

———. *Theology for Earth Community: A Field Guide.* Maryknoll, NY: Orbis Books, 1996.

Heyneman, Martha. *The Breathing Cathedral.* San Francisco: Sierra Club Books, 1993.

Hillman, James. *The Soul's Code—In Search of Character and Calling.* New York: Random House, 1996.

Hindley-Smith, Lea. *Secret Places.* Book 1 of *La Covenir, A Trilogy from the Summonsa Tapestries.* Toronto: A Therafield Book, 1976.

Horton, Myles, and Paulo Freire. *We Make the Road by Walking.* Philadelphia: Temple University Press, 1990.

Horwitt, Sanford. *Let Them Call Me Rebel.* New York: Alfred Knopf, 1989.

Industrial Areas Foundation. *I.A.F.—50 Years Organizing for Change.* New York: Franklin Square, 1990.

Ingram, Catherine. *In the Footsteps of Gandhi*. Berkeley: Parallax Press, 1990.

Jantsch, Erich. *The Self-Organizing Universe: Scientific and Human Implications of Emerging Paradigm of Evolution*, Tarrytown, NY: Pergaman Press, 1980.

Johnson, Elizabeth. *She Who Is*. New York: Crossroad Publishing, 1995.

———. *Spirit of Fire: The Life and Vision of Teilhard de Chardin*, Mystic, CT: Orbis Books, 1995.

Keen, Sam. *Hymns to an Unknown God*. New York: Bantam Books, 1994.

Kelly, Petra. *Thinking Green*. Berkeley, CA: Parallax Press, 1994.

Kelly, Tony. *An Expanding Theology*. Newton, New South Wales, Australia: E.J. Owyer, 1993.

King, Martin Luther, Jr. *I Have a Dream*. San Francisco: Harper San Francisco, 1993.

LaChance, Albert, and John Carroll, eds. *Embracing Earth—Catholic Approaches to Ecology*. Maryknoll, NY: Orbis Books, 1994.

Larson, Jean, Madge Cyrus, and Michael Cyrus. *Seeds of Peace*. Philadelphia, PA: New Society Publishers, 1987.

Leech, Kenneth. *The Eye of the Storm—Living Spiritually in the Real World*. San Francisco: Harper San Francisco, 1982.

Linfield, Michael. *The Dance of Change: An Eco-Spiritual Approach to Transformation*. New York: Routledge & Kegan Paul, 1986.

Lourde, Audre. *Sister Outsider: Essays and Speeches*. Freedom, CA. Crossing Press, 1984.

Mandela, Nelson. *Long Walk to Freedom*. London: ABACUS/Little Brown and Company, 1994.

May, Rollo. *My Quest for Beauty*. New York: Saybrook Publishing Company, 1985.

McBrien, Richard. *Catholicism*. Minneapolis: Winston Press, 1981.

McDaniel, Jay. *Earth Sky Gods and Mortals: A Theology of Ecology for the 21st Century*. Mystic, CT: Twenty-Third Publications, 1994.

———. *With Roots and Wings: Christianity in an Age of Ecology and Dialogue*. Maryknoll, NY: Orbis Books, 1995.

McDonagh, Sean. *Passion for Earth*. Maryknoll, NY: Orbis Books, 1995.

Merchant, Carolyn. *Radical Ecology—The Search for a Liveable World*. New York: Routledge, 1992.

———. *Earthcare*. New York: Routledge, 1995.

Merchant, Carolyn, ed. *Ecology*. Atlantic Highlands, NJ: Humanities Press, 1994.

Merton, Thomas. *Conjectures of a Guilty Bystander*. Garden City, NY: Doubleday, 1966.

———. *Contemplation in a World of Action*. London, Boston, Sydney: Mandala Books, Unwin Paperbacks, 1980.

———. *Preview of the Asian Journey*. Edited by William Capps. New York: Crossroad, 1989.

Miller, Ronald, and editors of *New Age Journal*. *As Above So Below*. Los Angeles: Jeremy Tarcher, 1992.

Mindell, Arnold. *Sitting in the Fire*. Portland, OR: Lao Tse Press, 1995.

Mooney, Christopher. *Teilhard de Chardin and the Mystery of Christ*. New York: Harper and Row, 1964.

Moore, Thomas. *Soul Mates*. New York: HarperCollins, 1994.

Nolan, Albert. *God in South Africa*. Grand Rapids, MI: William B. Eerdmanns, 1988.

Oelschlaeger, Max. *Caring for Creation: An Ecumenical Approach to the Environmental Crisis*. New Haven, CT: Yale University Press, 1994.

Padovano, Anthony. *Thomas Merton: Becoming Who We Are*. Cincinnati, OH: St. Anthony Messenger, 1995.

Pieris, Aloysius S.J. *An Asian Theology of Liberation*. Maryknoll, NY: Orbis Books, 1988.

Plant, Judith, ed. *Healing the Wounds: The Promise of Ecofeminism*. Philadelphia, PA: New Society Publishers, 1995.

Purple, David. *The Moral and Spiritual Crisis in Education*. Westport, CT: Birgen & Garvey, 1989.

Rae, Eleanor. *Women, Earth, the Divine*. Maryknoll, NY: Orbis Books, 1994.

Reich, Wilhelm. *The Murder of Christ*. New York: Noonday Press, 1970.

Reuther, Rosemary Radford, ed. *Women Healing Earth*. Maryknoll, NY: Orbis Books, 1996.

Rockefeller, Stephen, ed. *Spirit and Nature*. Boston: Beacon Press, 1992.

Rodgers, Mary Beth. *Cold Anger*. Denton, TX: University of North Texas Press, 1990.

Roszak, T., M. Gomes, and A. Kanner, eds. *Eco-Psychology: Restoring the Earth—Healing the Mind*. San Francisco: Sierra Club Books, 1995.

Roszak, Theodore. *The Voice of Earth*. New York: Simon & Schuster, 1992.

Ruether, Rosemary. *Womanguides: Readings Toward a Feminist Theology*. Boston: Beacon Press, 1996.

Schaef, Anne Wilson. *Beyond Therapy*. San Francisco: HarperSan Francisco 1992.

Schumacher, E.F. *A Guide for the Perplexed*. San Francisco: HarperSan Francisco, 1977.

Sessions, George, ed. *Deep Ecology for the 21st Century*. Boston/London: Shambala, 1995.

Shannon, William, ed. *Passion for Peace: The Social Essays of Thomas Merton.* New York: Crossroad Publishing, 1995.

Simpkinson, Charles, and Anne Simpkinson, eds. *Sacred Stories—A Celebration of the Power of Stories to Transform and Heal.* San Francisco: HarperSan Francisco, 1993.

Sismic, Wayne. *Praying with Thomas Merton.* Winona, MN: St. Mary's Press, 1994.

Skolimowski, Hendryk. *A Sacred Place to Dwell: Living with Reverence Upon Earth.* Rockport, MA: Element, Inc., 1993.

Soelle, Dorothee. *On Earth As in Heaven.* Louisville: Westminster/John Knox Press, 1993.

———. *Theology for Skeptics—Reflections on God.* Minneapolis: Augsburg Fortress Press, 1995.

Steindl-Rast, David, O.S.B. *The Music of Silence.* San Francisco/New York: HarperCollins, 1995.

Swimme, Brian. *The Hidden Heart of the Cosmos: Humanity and the New Story.* Maryknoll, NY: Orbis Books, 1996.

———. *The Universe Is a Green Dragon.* Santa Fe, NM: Bear & Co., 1984.

Tardiff, Mary, O.P., ed. *At Home in the World: The Letters of Thomas Merton and Rosemary Radford Reuther.* Maryknoll, NY: Orbis Books, 1995.

Tarnas, Richard. *The Passion of the Western Mind: Understanding the Ideas that Have Shaped our World View.* New York: Ballantine Books, 1991.

Teasdale, Wayne and George Cairns, eds. *The Community of Religions.* New York: Continuum, 1996.

Teilhard de Chardin, Pierre. *The Divine Milieu.* New York: Harper-Collins, 1960.

———. *The Heart of the Matter.* New York: Harcourt Brace, 1978.

Thich Nhat Hanh. *Being Peace.* Berkeley: Parallax Press, 1981.

———. *Be Still and Know.* New York: Riverhead Books, 1996.

Thompson, William Erwin. *Darkness and Shattered Light.* Garden City, NY: Anchor/Books, 1978.

Thornhill, John, S.M. *Christian Mystery in the Secular Age: The Foundation and Task of Theology.* Westminster, MD: Christian Classics, 1991.

Tickle, Phyllis. *Rediscovering the Sacred—Spirituality in America.* New York: Crossroad, 1995.

Tilby, Angela. *Science and the Soul.* London: SPCK, 1992.

Tilley, Terrence. *Postmodern Theology: The Challenge of Religious Diversity.* Maryknoll, NY: Orbis Books, 1995.

Tobias, Michael, and Georgianne Cowan. *The Soul of Nature—Visions of a Living Earth.* New York: Continuum, 1994.

Tokar, Brian. *The Green Alternative—Creating an Ecological Future.* San Pedro, CA: R. E. Miles, 1987.

Tucker, Mary Evelyn, and John Grim, eds. *World Views and Ecology: Religion, Philosophy and the Environment.* Maryknoll, NY: Orbis Books, 1994.

Wagoner, David. *Lost in the Forgotten Language: Contemporary Poets and Nature.* Edited by Christopher Morrill. Layton, UT: Peregrine Smith Books, 1991.

Wallis, Jim. *The Soul of Politics.* New York: The New Press, and Maryknoll, NY: Orbis Books, 1994.

———. *Who Speaks for God? An Alternative to the Religious Right—A New Politics of Compassion, Community and Civility.* New York: Delacorte Press, 1996.

Wheatley, Margaret. *Leadership and Science.* San Francisco: Barnett-Koehler Publications, 1992.

Wilder, Amos Niven. *Theopoetic: Theology and the Religious Imagination.* Minneapolis: Augsburg Fortress Press, 1976.

Woodman, Marion, and Elinor Dickson. *Dancing in the Flames.* Boston: Shamballa Publications, 1996.

Worthing, Mary William. *God, Creation, and Contemporary Physics.* Minneapolis: Augsburg Fortress Press, 1996.

Zohar, Danah, and Ian Marshall. *The Quantum Society: Mind, Physics and a New Social Vision.* New York: William Morrow & Co., 1994.

Notes

Prologue

1. Leonardo Boff, *The Path of Hope* (Maryknoll, NY: Orbis, 1993), 109.
2. Printed on the wall of the Starry Plough restaurant, Berkeley, CA.
3. Pierre Teilhard de Chardin, *The Divine Milieu* (New York: HarperCollins, 1960), 75.
4. Loren Eiseley, *Immense Journey* (New York: Vintage Books, 1959).
5. The articulation and development of these principles are found primarily in the works of Pierre Teilhard de Chardin and Thomas Berry.
6. Br. David Steindl-Rast, OSB. Unpublished, to my knowledge.

Embracing the Revelatory Moment

1. McGregor Smith, "Earth Literacy Link" (Environmental Ethics Institute, Wolfson Campus, Miami Dade Community College, Miami, FL).
2. Jay McDaniel, *With Roots and Wings: Christianity in an Age of Ecology and Dialogue* (Maryknoll, NY: Orbis Books, 1995).
3. Caroline Merchant, *Radical Ecology* (New York: Routledge, 1992). Adapted from "Where Are You? A Bioregional Quiz."
4. Thomas Berry and Brian Swimme, *The Universe Story* (San Francisco: Harper San Francisco, 1992), 25.
5. Ibid.
6. Ibid., 28.
7. McGregor Smith, "Earth Literacy Link."
8. Pierre Teilhard de Chardin, "The Phenomenon of Man," in *Discovery of Evolution* (New York: Harper & Brothers).
9. Mary Evelyn Tucker, "Education for Earth Literacy," *Earth Ethics* (Winter 1995).

In the Beginning Was the Dream

1. "Dream of Natashia Dzura," composed at a workshop conducted in Philadelphia, PA, summer 1995, unpublished and cited with permission.
2. Miriam MacGillis, personal communication, spring 1996.

Unfolding Mystery and Meaning

1. Thomas Berry, *Earth Story, Sacred Story* (Mystic CT: Twenty-Third Publications, 1994).
2. Thomas Berry and Brian Swimme, *The Universe Story*, 28.
3. Richard McBrien, *Catholicism* (New York: HarperCollins, 1981), 1058.
4. Thomas Berry, *Earth Story, Sacred Story*.
5. Charles Simpkinson and Anne Simpkinson, *Sacred Stories* (San Francisco: Harper San Francisco, 1993), chapter 19: Matthew Fox, "Stories That Need Telling Today," 244.
6. Matthew Fox, *Meditations with Meister Eckhart* (Santa Fe, NM: Bear & Co., 1982), 102.
7. Richard Harmon, unpublished manuscript (Mustard Seed, Brooklyn Ecumenical Cooperatives, 1986).
8. "World Views and Ecology," in *Ecological Geography*, Mary Evelyn Tucker and John Grim, eds. (Maryknoll, NY: Orbis Books, 1994), 233.
9. Clarissa Pinkola Estes, *100 Ways to Keep Your Soul Alive* (San Francisco: Harper San Francisco, 1994), also in *Women Who Run with Wolves* (New York: Ballantine, 1992).
10. Thomas Berry and Brian Swimme, *The Universe Story*, 25.
11. Ibid.
12. Ibid., 28.
13. McGregor Smith, "Earth Literacy Link."
14. Pierre Teilhard de Chardin, "The Phenomenon of Man" in *Discovery of Evolution*, (New York: Harper & Brothers, 1959).
15. Mary Evelyn Tucker, "Education for Earth Literacy," *Earth Ethics* (Winter 1995).

Fueling Our Acts of Re-Creation

1. Saul Alinsky, "A Candid Conversation with a Feisty Radical Organizer," *ICUIS*, 922 (1972): 178–179.
2. Saul Alinsky, *Rules for Radicals* (Random House, New York: 1971), 116.
3. Saul Alinsky, *Reveille for Radicals* (New York: Vintage Books, 1969), 223.
4. Msgr. John Egan, Paper presented at Urban Training Center, Toronto, 1972.
5. James Conlon, "Through the Son's Eyes," unpublished manuscript, 1979.
6. Saul Alinsky, *Rules for Radicals*, 11.
7. Ibid., 4.
8. Ibid., 22.
9. Ibid., 15.
10. Ibid., 51.
11. Saul Alinsky, *Reveille for Radicals*, 206.
12. James Conlon, "A Psycho-Social Experiment for Change" (Project Demonstrating Excellence, Union Graduate School, Cincinnati, 1975), 51
13. Saul Alinsky, *Reveille for Radicals*, 186.

14. Ibid., 186.
15. Ibid.
16. Saul Alinsky, *Rules for Radicals*, xxi.
17. Saul Alinsky, *Reveille for Radicals*, 226.
18. Saul Alinsky, *Rules for Radicals*, 13 (footnote).
19. Ibid., 92.
20. Ibid., 66.
21. Ibid.
22. Ibid., 93.
23. Saul Alinsky: "A Candid Conversation with a Feisty Radical Organizer," *ICUIS*, 922 (1972): 60.
24. Saul Alinsky, *Rules for Radicals*, 129.
25. Ibid.
26. James Conlon, "A Project for Social Change," unpublished manuscript, 1972.
27. Saul Alinsky, *Reveille for Radicals*, xiii.
28. Ibid., 61.
29. Saul Alinsky, *Rules for Radicals*, 61.
30. Ibid., 65.
31. Saul Alinsky, *Reveille for Radicals*, 175.
32. Saul Alinsky, *Rules for Radicals*, 20–21.
33. James Conlon, "A Psycho-Social Experiment for Change," 88.
34. Saul Alinsky, *Reveille for Radicals*, 15.
35. Ibid., 16, 17.
36. Ibid., 64.
37. Ibid., 197.
38. James Conlon, "Project for Social Change," 103.
39. Saul Alinsky, *Rules for Radicals*, 66.
40. Industrial Areas Foundation Saul Alinsky Training Institute brochure.
41. Saul Alinsky, *Reveille for Radicals*, 204.
42. Saul Alinsky, *Rules for Radicals*, 22.
43. Saul Alinsky, *Reveille for Radicals*, 206.
44. Saul Alinsky, *Rules for Radicals*, xxi.
45. Margaret Wheatley, *Leadership and the New Science* (San Francisco: Bennett-Koehler, 1992), 105.
46. Paulo Freire, *Education as the Practice of Liberty* (Geneva, Switzerland, Intitute for Culturel Action, 1970), 226.
47. Seminar on Community Education and Development (Class notes, Ontario Institute for Studies in Education, University of Toronto, 1976, 1).
48. Paulo Freire, *Education as the Practice of Liberty*, 278.
49. Paulo Freire, *Political Literary Process* (Geneva, Switzerland, Intitute for Culturel Action, 1970).
50. Alfred Hennelly, ed., *Santo Domingo and Beyond* (Maryknoll, NY: Orbis Books, 1993).
51. Seminar on Community Education and Development (Class notes).
52. Paulo Freire, *Education as the Practice of Liberty*, 278.

53. Paulo Freire, *Education for Critical Consciousness* (New York: Seabury Press, 1973), 9, 10.
54. Gregory Baum, *Man Becoming* (New York: Herder and Herder, 1970).
55. Theodore Roszak, *The Voices of Earth* (New York: Simon and Schuster, 1992).
56. Lecture by Dr. Allen Kanner, Holy Names College, Fall 1995.
57. Quoted in Matthew Fox, *Original Blessing* (Santa Fe, NM: Bear and Co., 1983).
58. Michael Tobias, ed., *Deep Ecology* (San Diego, CA: Avant Books, 1984), p. vii.
59. Lisa Faithorn, lecture given at Holy Names College, Fall 1995.
60. Andrew Dobson, ed., *The Green Reader* (San Francisco: Mercury House, 1991).
61. Joseph Campbell, *A Joseph Campbell Companion*, Diane Olson, ed. (New York Harper Collins, 1991).
62. Msgr. Jack Egan, in James Conlon, *Geo-Justice: A Preferential Option for Earth* (Woodlake Books, Winfield, B.C., Canada; San Jose, CA: Resource Publications, 1990; adapted from commentary for cover).
63. National Staff of Environmental Action, ed., *Earth Day—The Beginning* (New York: Arro Press, Bantam Books, 1970), xli.
64. Interview with Miriam MacGillis, *Creation Spirituality* magazine, Vol. x, No. iii, Autumn 1994, p. 15, Oakland, CA.
65. Gregory Baum and Duncan Cameron, *Ethics and Economics: Canada's Catholic Bishops on the Economic Crisis* (Toronto: James Larimer and Co., 1984), 67.
66. Robert Muller, quoted in Michael Linfield, *The Dance of Change* (New York: Routledge & Kegan Paul, 1989), 146.
67. "*Spiders,*" Elizabeth Johnson. Audio tape presentation with Thomas Berry.
68. Sally Helgensen, *Web of Inclusion* (New York: Currency/Doubleday, 1995).
69. *Training and Transformation: A Handbook for Community Workers*, Vol. 3 (Gweru, Zimbabwe: Mambo Press, 1985).
70. Dom Helder Camara, *Sister Earth—Ecology & Spirit* (London, New City, 1990).
71. Thomas Berry, *Dream of the Earth* (San Franscisco: Sierria Books, 1988).
72. Leonardo Boff, *Ecology and Liberation: A New Paradigm* (Maryknoll, NY: Orbis Books, 1995), 70.

Free Beyond All Measure

1. Marianne Williamson, *A Return to Love* (San Francisco: Harper San Francisco, 1993).
2. Thomas Merton, *Conjectures of a Guilty Bystander* (Doubleday Garden City, NY: 1996), 146.
3. Pierre Teilhard de Chardin, *Divine Milieu* (New York: Harper Collins, 1960), 75.

4. Thomas Merton, *Conjectures of a Guilty Bystander.*
5. From display card at Martin Luther King, Jr., Center, Atlanta, GA.
6. Miriam MacGillis, Workshop at Genesis Farm, summer 1995.

Epilogue

1. Sanskrit poem on display in La Paz, Bolivia.
2. Arthur Zajonc, *Catching the Light* (New York: Oxford University Press, 1995).
3. Interview with Miriam MacGillis, *Creation Spirituality* magazine, Vol. x, No. iii, Autumn 1994, p. 15, Oakland Ca.
4. Thomas Moore, *Care of the Soul* (New York: Harper Collins, 1992), xviii.

Lyrics for Music of the Universe

Peace, joy, happiness
Surprise, puppies, moonlight
Phone calls, meadows, rivers, night sky
Long walks, poems, drumming
Family, forgiveness, bridges, cars
Atone-ness, music, pumpkins
Oceans, beauty, patience, possibility
Memories, pain, candles, music
Laughter, tears, books, gentleness
Sunrise, flowers, rain, sunset, tears
Breeze, sunlight, solitude, darkness
Intimacy, leisure, knowing, trust
Think freely, smile
Tell those you love, that you do
Rediscover old friends, make new ones
Hope, dream, grow, give
Pick daisies, share them, laugh heartily
Act boldly, let someone in
Befriend a child, celebrate
Trust, believe, enjoy
Learn and discover as you
Listen to the music of the universe.